For **Times**
and for
Seasons

For Times and for Seasons

Great Ideas for
Family Devotionals and Activities!

John-Charles Duffy

First Printing: August, 2002

International Standard Book Number:
0-88290-715-8

Horizon Publishers' Catalog and Order Number:
2001

Printed and distributed
in the United States of America by

& Distributors, Incorporated

Mailing Address:
P.O. Box 490
Bountiful, Utah 84011-0490

Street Address:
50 South 500 West
Bountiful, Utah 84010

Local Phone: (801) 295-9451
Toll Free: 1 (866) 818-6277
FAX: (801) 295-0196

E-mail: horizonp@burgoyne.com
Web Site: http://www.horizonpublishersbooks.com

Contents

Times of Our Lives

Times of Adversity

Introduction

A Place of Devotion

"The key to strengthening our families," Elder Robert D. Hales reminds us, "is having the Spirit of the Lord come into our homes" (*Ensign*, May 1999, p. 33). Like our churches and temples, our homes can be houses of God—places of worship and spiritual reflection. As Elder Dean L. Larsen has explained, "[O]ur churches are not the only places where we can worship. Our homes should also be places of devotion" (*Ensign*, Nov. 1989, p. 63).

A home becomes a place of devotion when family members take time out to focus on things of the Spirit. Just as church members are strengthened by meeting together periodically, so too family members can "meet together oft, to fast and to pray, and to speak with one another concerning the welfare of their souls" (Moroni 6:5). Such gatherings give family members opportunties to support and nurture one another, to seek God's guidance in solving family problems, and to invite the Spirit into family celebrations. These kinds of gatherings are often referred to as family devotionals.

There is no one way to hold a family devotional. It might take the form of a family home evening, or it might consist simply of sharing a brief thought before family prayer. A family devotional might be held in the living room, around the dinner table, or on a bed. It might be relatively spontaneous, or it might involve careful preparation. Whatever form it takes, a family devotional is a time for family members to engage in spiritual reflection and to invite God's presence into their lives.

How to Use this Book

The purpose of this book is to help LDS families plan devotionals which apply the wealth of spiritual resources found in the Restoration to various family needs. The devotional ideas in this book are organized around different times when families might feel a special desire to invite the Spirit into their home or to teach gospel principles: times of the year (holidays and commemorations), times of our lives (major life events), and times of adversity.

Because a family devotional might take various forms, I have tried to include a variety of ideas, or ideas that could be adapted to a variety of circumstances: a brief reflection before family prayer, a discussion around the dinner table, a family scripture study session, a family council, or a family home evening. As you plan family devotionals, keep in mind King Benjamin's counsel not to run faster than you have strength (Mosiah 4:27). A family devotional should never feel like a burden or a chore. The quality of time, not the quantity of time, is what counts most.

In compiling ideas for family devotionals, I have been sensitive to the fact that families come "in a variety of appearances" (Thomas S. Monson, *Ensign*, Nov. 2000, p. 65). I have tried to use language broad enough to apply to different kinds of family structures: nuclear families, single-parent households, couples without children, households that include members of the extended family, or part-member families. Many of the ideas in this book could be adapted for use by single people as well.

It should be noted that this book is designed with a U.S. audience in mind. I trust that as the Church continues to grow internationally, Latter-day Saints in other countries and cultures will find ways to do in the context of their own traditions what I have tried to do here for U.S. holidays and customs.

Tips for Teaching

You will find that the lesson ideas and ideas for discussion included in this book typically consist of open-ended questions. I have not provided detailed "lesson plans" in order to emphasize how important it is that families seek the Spirit's inspiration in adapting the ideas in this book to their own circumstances.

At the same time, I realize that the task of creating a lesson or leading a discussion can feel overwhelming. The following tips may be useful.

Tips for Creating a Lesson

There are various ways you might develop the questions provided in the book into a lesson. You could simply gather as a family, read the scriptural passages listed, and discuss the questions spontaneously. But you may find that the following alternative approaches lead to more thoughtful, meaningful discussions.

• Provide family members in advance with a list of the scriptures and questions to be discussed. This approach, of course, gives family members more time to reflect in preparation for the devotional.

• Divide family members into groups. Assign each group a question. Have each group discuss their question among themselves and then report back to the rest of the family. This approach can get younger or quieter family members more involved in the devotional.

• Have family members respond to the questions in their journals. Invite family members to share some of what they have written, if they feel comfortable doing so. This approach invites family members to reflect more personally on the ideas raised in the devotional.

• Where multiple scriptures or questions are listed, choose just one scripture or one question to focus on in your family's discussion. This approach is useful when you want a shorter or more tightly focused devotional, or when you want to allow your family time to explore a question more deeply.

• Use the scriptures listed, but create your own set of questions to discuss. This approach lets you adapt the devotional more precisely to your family's needs.

• Instead of discussing the questions as a family, use them simply to help you prepare your lesson. See what ideas occur to you as you reflect on the questions. Then create a presentation that will explain those ideas to family members. This is an especially useful approach when creating lessons for young children.

Tips for Leading a Discussion

A discussion is generally a more effective teaching tool than a lesson where one person does all the talking. When people are actively engaged in a discussion, rather than passively listening to someone else speak, they will assimilate more of what is taught. Of course, the discussion must be adapted to family members' ages or capacities. Leading an effective discussion is something of a fine art, but the following pointers will help you get started.

• Consider giving family members questions to reflect on ahead of time. This will result in a more thoughtful discussion. It can also help draw quiet family members into the discussion.

• Use open-ended questions, rather than questions that have a right or wrong answer. An exception to this norm would be when you ask questions in order to review a concept or to check understanding in children. Even then, though, try to use prompts rather than questions ("Tell us about . . .").

• Give the person who is speaking your complete attention. Expect other family members to do the same (See D&C 88:122).

• If family members are brainstorming a list of some kind, write all their contributions down, in their own words. This shows family members that their ideas are taken seriously.

• Avoid passing judgment on family members' comments. Respect differences of opinion. Remind family members that there are various ways to apply gospel principles and that there is much we still do not know.

• Invite family members to expand on their comments, using prompts such as, "Tell us more about what you mean by that," or "What leads you to feel that way?"

• To prompt additional comments, ask, "What else?" (not "Anything else?" which implies that you want to move on).

• Avoid directing questions at individuals in a way that would make them feel they're being put "on the spot" or pressured to answer.

• Discussion may flow more freely if family members feel they are all on the same level—for instance, sitting in a circle. If the person leading the discussion is standing over everyone else, or in front of everyone else, that person will be seen as "having the floor," so others may contribute less.

Tips for Using the Scriptures

Family devotionals are an excellent opportunity to teach family members how to study and apply the scriptures. Consider the following suggestions for using the scriptures effectively and creatively.

• When you read a scripture, be sure to provide the necessary context. Who is speaking? To whom? Under what circumstances?

• As you look up passages, take the opportunity to help family members learn where different books of scripture are located. Use the songs which appear in The *Children's Songbook*, pp. 114, 116, and 119.

• After reading a passage of scripture, invite family members to paraphrase the passage in modern English. Take the time to discuss (or look up) difficult terms.

• Encourage family members to liken the scriptures to themselves by reading a passage aloud with their own names inserted where appropriate ("And when you, Suzanne, shall receive these things, I would exhort you . . .").

• In lieu of reading a story from the scriptures, retell it in your own words.

• Ask family members to prepare a re-enactment of a scriptural story. Family members might do this in person, with puppets, or even on video.

• Ask each family member to create a drawing to illustrate a passage of scripture used in the devotional. If the passage expounds doctrine, rather than telling a story, this may be challenging; encourage family members to be creative in approaching the task.

Tips for Involving Children

During her service as Primary General President, Michaelene P. Grassli urged adults to remember that "children have with all of us the divine right to spiritual enlightenment . . . Children can understand and should witness marvelous events, events like priesthood blessings, special ward and family fasts, the testimonies and prayers of their parents and leaders, and gospel discussions with people they love" (*Ensign*, Nov. 1992, p. 92, 93). Consider the following tips for involving children more fully in family devotionals.

• Children have a hard time understanding complex or multi-faceted ideas. Keep the devotional focused on a single, relatively simple concept.

• Children need time to process information. Slower explanations and repetition will be helpful.

• Children think in specific, concrete terms. The best way to help children understand gospel principles is to apply them to actual (not hypothetical) situations in life.

• Children think in terms of their own experiences; they have a hard time putting themselves in someone else's shoes. Rather than asking questions like, "How do you imagine someone would feel if . . . ?" ask, "Do you remember how you felt that time when . . . ?"

• Understanding symbols is a learned behavior. Since children tend to be literal-minded, they may have difficulty with the concept at first. If you use symbols, keep them simple and spell out their literal meaning.

• To a child's way of thinking, a thing is right or wrong simply because parents or teachers say so. Help your children begin to understand that we judge actions right or wrong based on how they affect ourselves and others.

• Changing activities frequently will help children stay focused. Also, you can keep children more engaged by having them adopt a more active role: asking them questions, inviting them to help with the presentation, and so on.

• While children need to learn to behave reverently when appropriate, a family devotional does not necessarily have to be somber or quiet to be spiritually meaningful. In the scriptures we find examples of people expressing devotion to God with laughter (Genesis 21:5-6), dancing (2 Samuel 6:14), clapping (Mosiah 18:11), shouting (2 Samuel 6:15; 3 Nephi 20:9; D&C 19:37), enthusiastic rejoicing (1 Nephi 1:14-15; Alma 27:17-18), and a "joyful noise" (Ps. 98:4).

• Use your family devotionals to reinforce the following basic gospel truths: Our Heavenly Father loves us unconditionally and wants us to be happy; Jesus is our example and is always available to help us; we are on earth to grow, learn, love, and serve.

Tips for Involving Adolescents

"Bring into the lives of our young people something more of spirituality," President Gordon B. Hinckley has exhorted (*Ensign*, Dec. 1995, p. 67). Family devotionals are a way of drawing on the power of the Spirit to help meet the special needs of adolescents. In addition, family devotionals give adolescents opportunities to teach the gospel and bear their testimonies. Consider the following ideas for making devotionals more engaging for family members in their teens.

• Adolescents are beginning to form opinions about relationships, politics, society, religion, and morality. Invite them to consider how gospel principles relate to the questions that matter to them.

• Challenge adolescents to move beyond clichés. Encourage them to probe beneath the surface of oft-repeated maxims ("What do we mean when we say . . . ?").

• Avoid presenting issues in oversimplified, black-and-white terms; adolescents are increasingly aware of the gray areas. Discuss real-life situations in which it is difficult to decide what to do or how to apply gospel principles.

• Keep in mind that adolescents are able to understand ideas in more complex terms, or to see an idea as having multiple dimensions: X is true, but so is Y. Paradoxes that would seem simply contradictory to children may be more meaningful for adolescents.

• As you discuss morality and agency with adolescents, avoid simply appealing to authority. Rather, show how moral standards and rules of conduct grow out of principles that ensure the well-being of all.

• Invite adolescents to take on greater responsibility for planning and conducting family devotionals.

• An adolescent may assert his/her independence by refusing to contribute to family devotionals. Enforce whatever family rules apply, but avoid a spirit of contention by being as flexible as possible within the limits created by the rules. For instance, would it be acceptable for your teen to attend the devotional without actively participating?

• Privacy is important to adolescents. You might want to ask an adolescent for permission before planning a devotional of which he/she will be the focus.

• In your devotionals, emphasize themes such as agency, personal spirituality, problem-solving, healthy relationships and lifestyles, moving into adulthood, meeting challenges with confidence, developing talents, and forming identity.

Tips for Involving Non-Members

Speaking of our relationships with people of other faiths, Elder M. Russell Ballard has said: "All our interpersonal relationships should be built on a foundation of mutual respect, trust, and appreciation. But that should not prevent us from sharing deeply held religious feelings with each other. Indeed, we may find that our [religious and] philosophical differences add flavor and perspective to our relationships" (*Ensign*, June 1998, p. 62; brackets in original). In that spirit, consider the following suggestions for involving non-LDS loved ones in your family devotionals.

• Be clear about your motives. If you give the impression that you are inviting people to participate in a spirit of interfaith sharing, but in fact you are planning to invite them to hear the missionary discussions, they are likely to feel deceived or used.

• Keep in mind that the Spirit acts on people in its own time and in its own way. Cultivate an environment where the Spirit can be present; then trust the Spirit to bring to pass whatever is meant to come to pass.

• Explain to non-LDS loved ones in advance what the devotional will consist of, so they know what to expect and so they can decide to what degree they would be comfortable participating.

• Build on common beliefs wherever possible. At the same time, there is no need to feel reticent or awkward about what is distinctively LDS. Surely your non-LDS loved ones expect to see something distinctive.

• If you are worried about how to explain distinctive LDS beliefs and practices without sounding preachy or pushy, try using the word "faith" or "tradition." For example: "In the LDS faith, baptism is administered at the age of eight." Or: "Our faith tradition describes God as the literal father of our spirits."

• Try focusing on broadly relevant themes such as love for God and neighbor, the importance of family, personal integrity, and service to others.

• Find ways in which non-LDS loved ones can actively contribute to the devotional. For instance, a non-LDS Christian relative might be invited to share his/her feelings about the Savior. A relative with no particular religious commitment might nevertheless be able to speak meaningfully on, say, the importance of serving other people or having personal standards.

Remembering the Savior

Sundays

Songs and Hymns

To Think About Jesus (*Children's Songbook* 71)
The Sacrament (*Children's Songbook* 72)
Remember the Sabbath Day (*Children's Songbook* 155)
When I Go to Church (*Children's Songbook* 157)
Gently Raise the Sacred Strain (*Hymns* 146)
Sabbath Day (*Hymns* 148)
Tis Sweet to Sing the Matchless Love (*Hymns* 176 or 177)
Welcome, Welcome, Sabbath Morning (*Hymns* 280)

Lesson Ideas

A. Hallowing the Sabbath

Exodus 19:9-11 (Six days shalt thou labor.)
Matthew 12:10-12 (It is lawful to do well on the Sabbath.)
D&C 59:13-14 (On this day do none other thing.)

• How can we make the Sabbath a joyful experience?
• How can we use the Sabbath as a day to do good?
• How can we use the Sabbath as an occasion to simplify our lives?

B. Jesus Rose the First Day

Psalms 118:21-24 (This is the day which the Lord hath made.)
Luke 24:1-3 or *John 20:1-2* (Jesus rose on the first day of the week.)
Acts 20:7 (On the first day of the week, the disciples broke bread.)

• Why did Jesus' followers find the day of his resurrection to be the most appropriate for worship?
• How does the Sabbath serve as a celebration of Christ's victory over sin and death?

• What is the value of setting aside one day each week to remember the atonement?

C. Preparing for the Sacrament

Revelation 7:17 (The Lamb shall feed them.)
3 Nephi 20:8-9 (Your soul shall never hunger nor thirst.)
Moroni 4-5 or *D&C 20:75-79* (The sacramental prayers.)
• What is the value of renewing our covenants every week?
• How is the sacrament a source of spiritual nourishment?
• How can we prepare ourselves for the sacrament?

Discussions and Activities

A. Read Exodus 23:21 and Mark 2:27. Make a list of ways that family members can use the Sabbath as a time for physical and spiritual renewal.

B. Read D&C 59:9-12. Discuss the following questions:
• What does it mean to "offer up" a sacrament?
• In what ways do we "pay devotion" during church meetings?
• What "oblations" do members of our family offer on Sundays?
• In what sense do Latter-day Saints today confess their sins to God and each other during church meetings?

C. Read Moroni 6:5 and D&C 1:19-23. Discuss the questions: In what sense might meetings be better if speakers and teachers in the restored church were required to receive formal training, as in many other denominations? What does the restored church gain by not having such a requirement? What would be a Christlike response to tedious speakers or inexpert teachers?

D. Invite family members to recount how the sacrament has been a source of spiritual nourishment for them.

E. Reread the baptismal covenant as found in Mosiah 18:8-10. Invite family members to reflect during the sacrament on how well they are living out that covenant.

F. Read 3 Nephi 18:28-30; Alma 38:14; and 1 John 3:18-21. Discuss the question: What do we learn from these scriptures about what it means to be worthy to take the sacrament?

G. Read Mark 10:13-14; Matthew 21:15-16; and 3 Nephi 17:23-24. Note that Jesus made a special effort to reach out to children during his ministry. Discuss the question: What can we do to help younger members of our family have a more meaningful spiritual experience in sacrament meeting?

H. To avoid a hectic—and spiritually disruptive—Sunday morning, consider using Saturday evening to do such things as ironing clothes, shining shoes, and finalizing preparations for talks or lessons. Indeed, you might find it useful to treat Saturday evening as part of your family's Sabbath observance.

I. Read Exodus 35:3. Propose to your family that in the spirit of this passage, and in the interest of practicing wise stewardship, family members make an effort to use less energy on the Sabbath. Take shorter showers. Plan meals that require little or no cooking. If your local meetinghouse is close, walk rather than drive.

J. Consider developing the custom of praying as a family immediately before leaving for church. Give thanks for the ways in which church attendance blesses or challenges family members. Especially give thanks for the opportunity to partake of the sacrament. Pray that the day's meetings will be a source of spiritual nourishment.

K. Suggest that family members develop the custom of writing briefly in their journals each Sunday after returning from church. They might record their feelings about that day's meetings, spiritual experiences or insights they had during church, or personal goals they set during the sacrament.

L. Resolve to include regular mention of the atonement and resurrection in your family's Sunday dinner prayer.

M. As a family, honor the Sabbath by performing service for someone in need.

Christmas

Songs and Hymns

In addition to those songs and hymns which are obviously for Christmas, the following may be appropriate, depending on the theme of the lesson:

When He Comes Again (*Children's Songbook* 82)
Where Love Is (*Children's Songbook* 138)
Come, Thou Glorious Day of Promise (*Hymns* 50)

Come, O Thou King of Kings (*Hymns* 59)
Come, Ye Disconsolate (*Hymns* 115)
How Long, O Lord Most Holy and True (*Hymns* 126)
Because I Have Been Given Much (*Hymns* 219)

Lesson Ideas

A. Prepare the Way of the Lord

Isaiah 40:1-5 (Prepare ye the way of the Lord, a highway for our God.)

Helaman 14:1-9 (Samuel the Lamanite urged the people to prepare the way.)

D&C 65 (Prepare ye the way of the Lord, make his paths straight.)

• How do we help prepare the way for the Lord's coming?

• How can we prepare for a spiritually rejuvenating Christmas celebration?

• What resolutions can we make for the coming year which will bring the Savior more fully into our lives?

B. The Condescension of God

1 Nephi 11:1-23 (Nephi's vision of the condescension of God.)

D&C 138:1-3 (God's love was manifest in the coming of the Redeemer.)

1 John 4:9-11 (In this was manifested God's love toward us.)

• Why was Nephi's vision of the tree of life accompanied by a vision of Christ's birth?

• How does our family's Christmas celebration help us feel God's love?

• How can we spread God's love abroad during this Christmas season? (see 1 Nephi 11:22)

C. Christ Came to Heal

Malachi 4:2 or *3 Nephi 25:2* (The Son shall arise with healing in his wings.)

Mosiah 3:1-8 (King Benjamin foresaw that Christ would come to heal.)

Alma 7:7-12 (Christ took our pains upon himself.)

• In what ways does Christ bring healing to our lives and to our world?

- When have members of our family experienced the Savior's healing influence?
- What can we do this Christmas to help bring that influence into others' lives?

D. God's Promises Are Fulfilled

3 Nephi 1:1-20 (Christ came into the world to fulfil the prophets' words.)

D&C 58:31 (Who am I that have promised and have not fulfilled?)

Jeremiah 33:14-15 (I will perform that good thing which I have promised.)

- How was Christ's birth a sign that our Heavenly Father fulfils his promises?
- What promises has our family received from God?
- How does our Christmas celebration bear witness to our faith that those promises will be fulfilled?

E. Unto You Is Born a Savior

Isaiah 9:2, 6-7 or *2 Nephi 19:2-3, 6-7* (Unto us a child is born.)

Isaiah 61:1-2 (Isaiah prophesied of the Savior's mission.)

Luke 2:1-20 (The angels announced the Savior's birth.)

- What did Isaiah prophesy the Savior would come to do?
- In what ways does our family help the Savior carry out his mission?
- In what ways have members of our family felt Christ's saving power in their lives?

F. Our Gifts for Christ

Matthew 2:1-12 (The wise men gave gifts to the Christ child.)

Mosiah 2:34 (Render to God all that you have and are.)

D&C 42:29-30, 38 (Inasmuch as ye do it unto the least of these.)

- What gifts can we each offer Christ during the course of the coming year?
- How do you imagine the wise men's experience affected them after they had returned to their homes and their everyday lives?
- How can we keep the Christmas spirit with us as we resume our everyday lives?

Discussions and Activities

A. Sit down as a family during the Thanksgiving weekend to make a schedule of your various preparations for Christmas: purchasing gifts, sending cards, decorating the house, baking goodies, visiting relatives, attending community events, and so on. Mosiah 4:27 could provide a scriptural basis for this activity.

B. Use the Lesson Ideas suggested above to focus on a different dimension of the Christmas message during each of the four weeks between Thanksgiving and Christmas. For instance:

- *Week 1:* Prepare the Way of the Lord
- *Week 2:* The Condescension of God
- *Week 3:* Christ Came to Heal
- *Week 4:* God's Promises Are Fulfilled

C. In the spirit of D&C 93:53, research the Christmas customs of another country. You might choose a country from which your ancestors come, or a country where a family member has served a mission. Incorporate some of that country's customs into your family's Christmas celebration.

D. Taking 2 Nephi 9:51 as your inspiration, declare this year a "commercialism-free Christmas" for your family. Resolve that all gifts and cards exchanged between family members will be handmade, not store-bought. Engage in simple, low-cost holiday activities.

E. On the night of Christmas Eve, turn off all the lights in the house except for the lights on the Christmas tree and other holiday decorations. Gather family members around a lighted nativity scene. Read or tell the Christmas story. Then invite family members to share their thoughts or feelings about the Savior. (The lesson, "Unto You Is Born a Savior," would accomplish the same purpose.) Conclude by singing "Silent Night" and retiring to bed.

F. Before opening Christmas presents, take 10 minutes or so to read Matthew 2:1-2, 11; John 3:16-17; Romans 5:14-15; and 3 Nephi 14:7-11. Discuss the question: What gospel truths is the custom of Christmas gift-giving meant to remind us of?

G. Many people today celebrate the twelve days of Christmas by performing secret service projects on the 12 days leading up to December 25. Originally, however, the twelve days of Christmas were December 25 and the 11 days following. Consider reviving this older custom to make your family's Christmas celebration last longer. Plan a different service project for the twelve days following December 25.

H. In many parts of the Christian world—especially in the Spanish-speaking world— January 6 is the day used to commemorate the wise men's coming to worship the Christ child. In medieval times, January 6 was also the day which followed the twelve days of Christmas feasting. Consider using this date to mark the end of your family's Christmas celebration. Take down Christmas decorations on or shortly after this date, and use the lesson, "Our Gifts for Christ," as your family's final Christmas devotional.

Easter

Songs and Hymns

Did Jesus Really Live Again? (*Children's Songbook* 64)
He Died That We Might Live Again (*Children's Songbook* 65)
Hosanna (*Children's Songbook* 66)
Easter Hosanna (*Children's Songbook* 68)
Jesus Has Risen (*Children's Songbook* 70)
I Know That My Redeemer Lives (*Hymns* 136)
That Easter Morn (*Hymns* 198)
He Is Risen! (*Hymns* 199)
Christ the Lord Is Risen Today (*Hymns* 200)

Lesson Ideas

A. Hope in the Resurrection

Mosiah 16:6-9 (The risen Christ is a light that can never be darkened.)

Moroni 9:25 (May Christ's resurrection rest in your mind, to lift you up.)

1 Corinthians 15:55-58 (Know that your labor is not in vain.)

• In what ways can the resurrection be a source of hope?

• When has our faith in the resurrection given us strength, comfort, or vision?

• How have members of our family experienced the risen Christ's light in their lives?

B. We Go on Forever

Alma 41:2-3, 14-15 (That which we send out will be restored to us.)

D&C 88:27-31 (We will receive the same body and glory we received in life.)

D&C 130:2, 18-19 (Our relationships and intelligence will rise with us.)

• What do these passages teach us about the relationship between our life now and our life in the resurrection?

• What would someone "quickened by a portion of the celestial glory" be like (D&C 88:29)?

• How can we make our family one which we would want to be part of forever?

C. All Shall Be Made Alive

1 Corinthians 15:20-22 (In Christ shall all be made alive.)

2 Nephi 9:6-12 (The resurrection delivers us from death and hell.)

Helaman 14:15-17 (The resurrection redeemeth all from the first death.)

• According to Jacob (2 Nephi 9), how does the resurrection put an end to hell?

• How is the resurrection a demonstration of God's unconditional love?

• What practical difference does it make in our lives to know that death is not final?

D. Raised from Everlasting Death

Ephesians 2:4-7 (We were dead in sins; God hath quickened us with Christ.)

Colossians 3:1-2 (If ye are risen with Christ, seek those things which are above.)

2 Nephi 10:25 (God raises you from death and also from everlasting death.)

Mosiah 27:22-29 (Alma was snatched from spiritual death.)

• Why does Paul speak of the faithful as having already been raised with Christ?

• In what sense could it be said that Alma's conversion was a kind of resurrection?

• What is the process by which we are raised from spiritual death?

E. Newness of Life

Romans 6:3-8 (Those baptized are in the likeness of Christ's resurrection.)

Colossians 2:12-14 (Buried with Christ in baptism, wherein also ye are risen with him.)

Mosiah 18:8-10 (Alma's explanation of the baptismal covenant.)

• According to Paul, what is the connection between baptism and the resurrection?

• What are the terms of the baptismal covenant, as Alma taught them?

• How is it that in living this covenant we "walk in newness of life" (Romans 6:4)?

F. Risen Lord and Advocate

2 Nephi 2:8-9 (The risen Christ makes intercession for all.)

Mosiah 15:8-9 (The resurrection gave the Son power to make intercession.)

D&C 45:3-5 (The risen Christ's intercessory prayer.)

• What does it mean to say that Christ makes intercession for us?

• How did the resurrection give Christ the power to make intercession?

• How have family members experienced the Savior's mercy and love in their lives?

G. The Risen Christ Is over All

D&C 20:23-24 (Christ rose and ascended to reign with almighty power.)

Ephesians 1:19-23 (God hath put all things under Christ's feet.)

Romans 14:7-9 (Whether we live or die, we are the Lord's.)

• How did the resurrection give Christ power over all things?

• At times when we feel anxious or overwhelmed, what difference does it make to know that Christ has power over all?

• In what ways do we experience Christ's power in our lives?

H. Our Relationship with the Risen Christ

Matthew 28:16-20 (The risen Christ says, "I am with you always.")

John 20:19-21 (The risen Christ sends peace to his disciples.)

3 *Nephi 11:8-17* (The risen Christ had an individual encounter with each person.)

JS-H 1:15-17 (The risen Christ appeared to Joseph Smith.)

• When have members of our family felt Christ's peace and presence in their lives?

• How can we cultivate a personal relationship with the risen Christ?

• What is the risen Christ's role in the Restoration?

Discussions and Activities

A. A few weeks before Easter, hold personal interviews with each family member. Review their progress toward meeting their New Year's resolutions or other spiritual goals. Invite them to use the period between now and Easter to make a special effort to focus on their goals or to get back on track.

B. During the weeks leading up to Easter, use some of the Lesson Ideas suggested above to focus on various dimensions of the atonement and resurrection.

C. Sometime in the week before Easter, read or retell the story of Jesus' suffering in Gethsemane and his death at Calvary. Invite family members to reflect in their journals on the significance this story has for them, or on ways they experience Christ's atonement in their lives.

D. During the week before Easter, read and discuss the following passages of scripture, perhaps during a mealtime, when all family members can be present.

• **Sunday:** *Mark 11:1-11* (The triumphal entry.)

• **Monday:** *Mark 11:15-19* (Jesus cleanses the temple.)

• **Tuesday:** *Mark 12:28-34* and Matthew 25:31-46 (Jesus' last public teachings.)

• **Wednesday:** *Mark 14:3-11* (Jesus is anointed for burial.)

• **Thursday:** *Luke 22:7-71* (Last Supper and Gethsemane.)

• **Friday:** *Mark 15* (Jesus is crucified.)

• **Saturday:** *D&C 138:11-19* (Jesus visits the spirit prison.)

E. Assign each family member to make an Easter basket for someone else in the family. Each basket should include a letter for the person receiving the basket, describing ways in which the giver has seen that person living out the message of Easter. That might include:

- Ways the person demonstrates faith in the living Christ.
- Ways the person nurtures a personal relationship with the Savior.
- Ways the person exemplifies living with hope.
- Ways the person contributes to building an eternal family.
- Ways the person strives to "walk in newness of life" (Romans 6:4).
- Ways the person demonstrates an eternal perspective.

F. As a family, read the document, "The Living Christ: The Testimony of the Apostles." Ask family members to comment on statements from the declaration which stood out to them.

G. Invite family members to reflect silently on things that make them feel anxious, overwhelmed, or inadequate. Then read Matthew 12:38-40 and Jonah 1:17-2:10. Explain that as God delivered Jonah from the various forces that "compassed [him] about" (Jonah 2:3), so the resurrection has the power to deliver us from everything that might hold us back from achieving our eternal potential.

H. Invite family members to reflect (either silently or aloud) on events in the past year that hurt them or caused them sorrow. Read Isaiah 25:8. Discuss the question: How does the resurrection serve as God's answer to sorrow and pain?

I. As a family, compile a list of joys, or wholesome pleasures, that we experience in the physical world (good food, an embrace, a warm fire, a beautiful landscape). Read D&C 93:33-34. Point out that experiencing these kinds of joys is one of the purposes of earth life and of the resurrection.

J. Celebrate the resurrection through service to the needy. Plan a special family service project to be carried out on or near Easter.

Ideas for a Sunrise Service

In many parts of the Christian world, it is customary to gather in a cemetery early Easter morning for a sunrise service. Such a service affords participants an opportunity to reflect on the meaning of the resurrection in their lives. Consider the following suggested outline for a simple family sunrise service.

A. An opening song and prayer.

B. A few words of welcome to explain the purpose of the gathering and to set the tone for the service.

C. A reading or retelling of the story of the resurrection as found in the scriptures (for instance, John 20:1-18).

D. A prepared talk by a family member on the significance of the resurrection, or one of the Lesson Ideas above.

E. A time for family members to voice their thoughts or feelings about the resurrection.

F. Some simple closing remarks. This would be a good opportunity for the person leading the service to express his/her love for other family members and his/her hope that the family will be together forever.

G. A closing song and prayer.

Commemorating the Restoration

Joseph Smith's Birthday
(December 23)

Note: Since Joseph Smith's birthday may be eclipsed by Christmas, an alternative would be to remember him on the anniversary of his martyrdom, June 27.

Songs and Hymns

The Sacred Grove (*Children's Songbook* 87)
On a Golden Springtime (*Children's Songbook* 88)
Truth Eternal (*Hymns* 4)
Now We'll Sing with One Accord (*Hymns* 25)
Joseph Smith's First Prayer (*Hymns* 26)
Praise to the Man (*Hymns* 27)
A Poor Wayfaring Man of Grief (*Hymns* 29)

Lesson Ideas

A. Founder of a Great Work

D&C 21:1-2 (Inspired to lay the foundation of a most holy faith.)

D&C 64:33 (Ye are laying the foundation of a great work.)

D&C 135:3 (John Taylor's list of Joseph Smith's achievements.)

• How has the work which Joseph Smith began continued to grow?

• How does our family contribute to that work?

• How has the Restoration helped our family come closer to God?

B. A Latter-day Prophet

D&C 5:9-10 (This generation shall have my word through you.)

D&C 20:5-12 (God inspires men in this age as in generations of old.)

D&C 21:4-6 (His word ye shall receive as if from mine own mouth.)

• In what ways did Joseph Smith reaffirm ancient prophetic and apostolic teachings?

• What unique teachings were revealed through Joseph Smith?

• How have Joseph's teachings helped our family come closer to God?

C. A Witness of Christ

JS-H 1:15-17 (Joseph Smith's First Vision of the Father and the Son.)

D&C 76:22-23 (This is the testimony which we give of him.)

D&C 110:1-4 (Joseph Smith saw Jesus Christ in the Kirtland Temple.)

• What difference does it make to have a witness of Christ in modern times?

• What do Joseph Smith's revelations teach us about Christ?

• How has the Restoration helped our family draw closer to the Savior?

Discussions and Activities

A. Compile a list of teachings of Joseph Smith which have been meaningful to members of your family. Ask family members to explain why these teachings have been meaningful to them.

B. Read D&C 27:12-13. Discuss the questions: What gospel ordinances or keys were restored through Joseph Smith? How have those ordinances and keys helped our family draw closer to God?

C. Create a poster in the shape of a cloud. Attach to it pictures or scriptural quotations to represent various witnesses of Christ found in the scriptures (prophets, apostles, eye-witnesses to the resurrection). Finally, add Joseph Smith to the poster.

Then read Hebrews 12:1-2. Discuss the questions: How does having this "cloud of witnesses" strengthen our faith in Christ? What difference does it make to have a witness of Christ in our own day as well as in ancient times?

D. Read D&C 124:1. Discuss the questions: In what ways did Joseph Smith display weakness? What other examples can we find in the scriptures of people who were called by God despite their weakness? Why is it significant that the Lord calls "the weak things of the earth" to serve as his instruments?

E. Sing all seven verses of "A Poor Wayfaring Man of Grief" — twice. Explain that this was the last hymn Joseph Smith requested to hear sung in his life, and that it moved him so much he asked to have it sung twice. Discuss the question: Why would this particular hymn have been so meaningful to Joseph?

F. In the closing prayer, thank Heavenly Father for the contributions of Joseph Smith. Pray that the work he began will continue to bless the world.

Founding of the Relief Society
(March 17)

Songs and Hymns

I'm Trying to Be like Jesus (*Children's Songbook* 78)
I Want to Live the Gospel (*Children's Songbook* 148)
Because I Have Been Given Much (*Hymns* 219)
Lord, I Would Follow Thee (*Hymns* 220)
Love One Another (*Hymns* 308, *Children's Songbook* 136)
As Sisters in Zion (*Hymns* 309)
A Key Was Turned in Latter Days (*Hymns* 310)

Lesson Ideas

A. The Mission of the Relief Society

Colossians 3:12-17 (Put on charity, teach one another, do all things in the Lord's name.)

Mosiah 4:26-27 (Administer to the relief of the poor.)

D&C 82:14 (Zion must arise and put on her beautiful garments.)

• How do these passages relate to the mission of the Relief Society?

• How does the mission of the Relief Society relate to the mission of the Church?

• In what ways does the Relief Society carry out its mission?

B. Charity Never Faileth

1 Corinthians 13:1-8 (Charity never faileth.)

Moroni 7:47-48 (Charity is the pure love of Christ.)

D&C 88:125 (Above all things, clothe yourselves with charity.)

• What does it mean to say, "Charity never faileth"?

• What signs do we see that the world needs to learn greater charity?

• How does the Relief Society serve as a vehicle for rendering Christlike service?

C. Handmaids of the Lord

Luke 1:26-38, 46-49 (Mary was a handmaid of the Lord.)

• What does it mean to be a handmaid of the Lord?

• How do members of the Relief Society function as servants of the Lord?

• How can male members of the church support the Relief Society's work?

D. Building up God's Kingdom

Luke 12:29-34 (Seek the kingdom of God, not earthly treasures.)

Jacob 2:18-19 (Before ye seek for riches, seek for the kingdom of God.)

D&C 6:6-8 (You shall be the means of doing much good.)

• How do members of the Relief Society help build up God's kingdom?

• In what ways does the Relief Society do good in the world?

• How does the Relief Society provide opportunities for church members— male and female—to use their means to serve God and others?

Discussions and Activities

A. As a family, create a poster bearing the Relief Society seal. Underneath the seal, ask each family member to write a sentence, summarizing what the slogan "Charity Never Faileth" means to him or her.

B. Display a copy of the Relief Society Declaration. Invite family members—male and female—to testify about any of the following:

• How the gospel gives their lives "meaning, purpose, and direction."

• How prayer and scripture study have strengthened their testimonies of the Savior.

• How they strive to develop their full potential as children of God.

• The practices that bring them spiritual strength.

• The importance of supportive, nurturing family relationships.

• The satisfaction that comes from serving others.

• The role of priesthood ordinances, including temple ordinances, in their lives.

• Ways they have seen family members show their love for life.

• Ways they have seen family members stand for truth and righteousness.

C. Ask each family member to come to the devotional with at least one scriptural passage which describes something Jesus or his apostles did to build God's kingdom or help others. Discuss the question: In what ways does the Relief Society continue the work of Jesus and his apostles in modern times?

D. Ask a family member—preferably one who is a member of the Relief Society—to recount the story of how the Relief Society was founded. Discuss the question: How does the Relief Society in modern times continue to carry out its original mission?

E. Ask family members to prepare brief presentations on women from the scriptures who exemplify faith, virtue, vision, or charity. These include:

• *Eve:* set in motion the plan of happiness (Moses 4:7-12; 5:11).

• *Sarah:* entered into the Lord's covenant (Genesis 17:15-16).

• *Rebekah:* received personal revelation (Genesis 25:21-23).

• *Miriam:* a leader of the women of Israel (Exodus 15:20-21).

• *Ruth:* left her country to care for her widowed mother-in-law (Ruth 1).

- *Deborah:* served as a judge over Israel (Judges 4).
- *Hannah:* prayed for the Lord's help in her troubles (1 Samuel 1).
- *The wise woman of Tekoah:* served as a peacemaker (2 Samuel 14:1-20).
- *The widow of Zarephath:* trusted in God's power (1 Kings 8:16).
- *Huldah:* exhorted king Josiah to keep the covenant (2 Chronicles 34).
- *Esther:* risked her life in order to save her people (Esther 4).
- *Mary of Nazareth:* accepted God's mission for her (Luke 1:26-38).
- *Elizabeth:* received discernment from the Spirit (Luke 1:39-45).
- *Ana:* served God in the temple (Luke 2:36-38).
- *The Samaritan woman:* told her neighbors about Christ (John 4).
- *The widow in the temple:* gave everything she had (Mark 12:41-44).
- *Martha:* received the Lord into her home (Luke 10:38).
- *Mary of Bethany:* sought spiritual knowledge (Luke 10:39-42).
- *Mary Magdalene:* testified of the risen Lord (John 20:1-18).
- *Tabitha (Dorcas):* known for her good works (Acts. 9:36-42).
- *Priscilla:* an early missionary (Acts 18; Romans 16:3-4).
- *Phebe:* a servant of the church and a succorer of many (Romans 16:1-2).
- *Sarai:* left her home to fulfill God's will (1 Nephi 2).
- *The Lamanite queen:* commended for her faith (Alma 19:2-10).
- *Abish:* instrumental in bringing the gospel to the Lamanites (Alma 19).
- *The Ammonite mothers:* taught their children to trust God (Alma 56:45-48).
- *Emma Smith:* called to assist in the work of the Restoration (D&C 25).
- *Vienna Jacques:* called by the Lord to help build Zion (D&C 90:28-31).

F. As a family, make a financial contribution to the Relief Society's literacy project.

G. By an intriguing coincidence, the anniversary of the founding of the Relief Society falls in the same month as International Women's Day (March 8). In 1981 LDS senator Orrin Hatch cosponsored a resolution which declared the week surrounding March 8 to be "National Women's History Week."

During the month of March many colleges, libraries, and other civic institutions mount exhibits on the achievements and contributions of women. Your family might find it interesting to visit and discuss such exhibits. You might also find it interesting to research the history of the Relief Society's involvement in such areas as women's suffrage, education, and humanitarian work.

H. In the closing prayer, thank God for the ways in which the Relief Society blesses your family, the Church, and the world. Pray especially for family members who belong to the Relief Society (or who will one day belong to the Relief Society), that they will be effective instruments in God's hands.

Restoration of the Church
(April 6)

Songs and Hymns
The Church of Jesus Christ (*Children's Songbook* 77)
I'm Trying to Be like Jesus (*Children's Songbook* 78)
The Spirit of God (*Hymns* 2)
Awake and Arise (*Hymns* 8)
O Saints of Zion (*Hymns* 39)
Lord, I Would Follow Thee (*Hymns* 220)
Have I Done Any Good? (*Hymns* 223)

Lesson Ideas
A. Blessings of the Restoration
D&C 1:17-28 (I called upon my servant Joseph Smith.)

• According to these verses, what were the objectives of the Restoration?

• In what ways do Latter-day Saints today work towards these objectives?

• In what ways has the Restoration blessed our family?

B. A Nurturing Community

Acts 2:44-47 (All that believed were together.)
Moroni 6:4-6 (The church did meet together oft.)
D&C 88:122-123 (See that ye love one another.)

• How did church members support one another in ancient times?

• How has membership in the restored church nourished our family?

• How does our family serve and support other church members?

C. A Force for Good

Acts 10:37-38 (Jesus went about doing good.)
Alma 1:29-30 (Members of the church gave liberally to all.)
3 Nephi 27:21 (Do the works which ye have seen me do.)

• How does the restored church carry out the works of Jesus in the world?

• In what ways do members of our family participate in that work?

• How has the Restoration inspired our family to do good outside church circles?

D. Building up Zion

Isaiah 14:32 or *2 Nephi 24:32* (The poor shall trust in Zion.)
D&C 12:6-8 (Seek to establish the cause of Zion.)
D&C 58:6-12 (Zion will bring all people to the Lord's feast.)
Moses 7:18 (Why the Lord called his people Zion.)

• What do these passages teach us about what it means to build up Zion?

• How did early members of the restored church attempt to build up Zion?

• How can church members today live true to this Zion-building heritage?

Discussions and Activities

A. Review the three-fold mission of the Church. Compile a list of ways family members contribute to the Church's mission. Discuss the question: How have family members been blessed through this work? How have they been able to bless others?

B. Read D&C 20:1-28. Make a list of the basic beliefs of the restored church, as they are laid out in these verses. Invite family members to testify about the importance of these beliefs in their own lives.

C. As a family, create a collage depicting various ways in which family members do the works of Jesus, either in church circles or in the world at large. Title the collage "We are the body of Christ" (see 1 Corinthians 12:27).

D. Hold a "birthday party" for the restored church. Consider the following ideas:

• Decorate your home with balloons, or with banners bearing slogans from some of the scriptures used in the Lesson Ideas above.

• Have a special meal, with cake afterwards.

• Retell the story of the restoration of the Church.

• Ask each family member to prepare a "birthday gift" for the Church by pledging to contribute in some special way to the Church's mission.

• As a family, make an extra financial gift to the Church, or perform some kind of service at the local meetinghouse.

E. In the closing prayer, give thanks for the blessings that have come to your family through the Restoration. Ask God to continue to guide the restored church as it carries out Christ's work in the world. Pray for the well-being of all church members.

Restoration of the Priesthood
(May 15)

Songs and Hymns

I'm Trying to Be like Jesus (*Children's Songbook* 78)
The Priesthood is Restored (*Children's Songbook* 89)
I Want to Live the Gospel (*Children's Songbook* 148)

I Will Be Valiant (*Children's Songbook* 162)
Come, Sing to the Lord (*Hymns* 10)
Lord, I Would Follow Thee (*Hymns* 220)
Thy Servants Are Prepared (*Hymns* 261)
Brightly Beams Our Father's Mercy (*Hymns* 335)

Lesson Ideas

A. The Mission of the Priesthood

John 21:15-17 (Jesus charged Peter to feed his sheep.)

JS-H 1:68-71 (John the Baptist restored the Aaronic priesthood.)

D&C 27:12-13 (Peter, James, and John restored the Melchizedek priesthood.)

D&C 84:19-21 (Through the priesthood, God's power is manifest.)

D&C 107:18-20 (The power of the Melchizedek and Aaronic priesthoods.)

• What do these passages teach us about the priesthood's mission?

• In what sense is the priesthood's mission the mission of all church members?

• How do priesthood ordinances bring God's love and presence into people's lives?

B. The Service of God

Matthew 25:34-40 (The parable of the sheep and the goats.)

Mosiah 2:17 (To serve your fellow beings is to serve God.)

D&C 81:5 (Stand in your office: strengthen the feeble knees.)

• What do we learn from these passages about what it means to serve God?

• How do priesthood ordinances impart spiritual strength to church members?

• How does the priesthood empower all church members (not only priesthood holders) to serve God and others?

C. Ordained to Be Servants

Matthew 24:45-51 or *JS-M 1:49-54* (Faithful and unfaithful servants.)

Luke 22:24-27 (To hold Christ's authority is to serve.)

D&C 121:34-46 (Priesthood holders are warned against unrighteous dominion.)

• How does the priesthood empower all church members (not only priesthood holders) to serve the Lord?

• What do we learn from these passages about the qualities of a faithful servant?

• How has our family been served or blessed by the priesthood?

D. Building up God's Kingdom

Luke 12:29-34 (Seek the kingdom of God, not earthly treasures.)

Jacob 2:18-19 (Before ye seek for riches, seek for the kingdom of God.)

D&C 6:6-8 (You shall be the means of doing much good.)

• How does the priesthood empower all church members (not only priesthood holders) to build up the kingdom?

• What does it mean to build up God's kingdom on earth?

• How do members of our family use their means to serve God and others?

Discussions and Activities

A. Ask each family member to come to the devotional with at least one scriptural passage which describes something Jesus or his apostles did to build God's kingdom or help others. Discuss the question: In what ways does the priesthood empower members of the restored church to continue the work of Jesus and his apostles in modern times?

B. Read 1 Corinthians 12:4-6, 12-18 and D&C 46:10-12. Discuss the following questions:

• In what different ways do members of our family serve others, both in the Church and in the world at large?

• How does the service we render help to strengthen the body of Christ and make the world a better place?

• How do all these different kinds of service contribute to the mission of the priesthood?

C. Read D&C 12:6-8. Discuss the question: Why does the Lord trust mere mortals to carry out his work? Ask family members to recount instances when they have seen people demonstrate the qualities listed in this passage of scripture (humble, full of love, etc.).

D. If there is a priesthood holder in your family, ask him to show how his line of authority goes back to the appearance of Peter, James, and John to Joseph Smith and Oliver Cowdery. Discuss the question: What difference does it make to know that we have in our home a priesthood which comes down to us from the Savior himself?

E. Read Exodus 19:5-6; 1 Peter 2:5; 1 Nephi 14:14; and D&C 49:9. Discuss the questions: How did the restoration of the priesthood make it possible for members of the restored church to be a covenant people? What does it mean to be a covenant people?

F. Ask family members to think of stories from the Bible and the Book of Mormon that show people doing good through God's power. Discuss the question: What difference does it make to know that members of the restored church have access to the same power which the prophets and saints in ancient times used to carry out God's work?

G. As a family, list as many blessings as you can think of that have come to your family through the priesthood: gospel ordinances, revealed teachings, opportunities for service, even the earth itself. Give thanks for these things in the closing prayer.

Pioneer Day
(July 24)

Songs and Hymns

Pioneer Children Sang As They Walked (*Children's Songbook* 214)

Westward Ho! (*Children's Songbook* 217)
To Be a Pioneer (*Children's Songbook* 218)
The Handcart Song (*Children's Songbook* 220)
Covered Wagons (*Children's Songbook* 221)
High on the Mountain Top (*Hymns* 5)
Come, Come, Ye Saints (*Hymns* 30)
O God, Our Help in Ages Past (*Hymns* 31)
They, the Builders of the Nation (*Hymns* 36)

Lesson Ideas
A. God Delivered Our Forebears
Psalms 105:1-5, 39-41 (Remember his marvelous works.)

Alma 36:2-3 (Remember the captivity of our fathers.)

D&C 136:22 (I am he who led the children of Israel out of Egypt.)

• How did God help the Israelites as they traveled to the promised land?

• How did God help the pioneers as they traveled west?

• What difference does this knowledge make in our own lives?

B. A Heritage of Faith
D&C 58:3-5 (Ye cannot behold now the design of God.)

D&C 78:18 (I will lead you along.)

D&C 136:1-4 (We will walk in all the ordinances of the Lord.)

• How did the pioneers demonstrate trust in God?

• How does our family demonstrate trust in God?

• How does our family walk in the ordinances of the Lord?

C. Building up Zion
D&C 12:6-8 (Seek to establish the cause of Zion.)

D&C 136:10 (The pioneers were sent to build up Zion.)

Moses 7:18 (Why the Lord called his people Zion.)

• What do these passages teach us about what it means to build up Zion?

• How did the pioneers help to build up Zion?

• How can our family help establish the cause of Zion in today's world?

D. An End to Persecutions
Psalms 133 (How pleasant it is to dwell together in unity!)

Mosiah 27:2-4 (There should be no persecutions.)

D&C 136:34 (Thy brethren have driven you out.)

• Why did the pioneers have to flee west?

• What examples of intolerance or persecution do we see in today's world?

• How can people with different beliefs and values learn to live together?

E. Gathered from among the Nations

Isaiah 2:2-3 or *2 Nephi 12:2-3* (All nations shall flow to the Lord's house.)

D&C 38:27 (If ye are not one, ye are not mine.)

D&C 45:71 (The righteous shall be gathered from all nations.)

• How did the Church's pioneer era bring together people from various nations?

• How does the Church continue to bring together people from various nations?

• How is the Church both blessed and challenged by this diversity?

Discussions and Activities

A. Read Isaiah 2:22 or 2 Nephi 12:22. Discuss the question: Why do we set aside a day to honor pioneers? What is the appropriate tone for such an observance?

B. Read D&C 136 in its entirety. Discuss the question: How does the counsel given in this revelation to the pioneers apply to us today?

C. Use a dictionary or thesaurus to arrive at a broad sense of the meaning of the word "pioneer." Discuss the question: Given this broad definition, in what ways do members of our family serve as pioneers?

D. Read the following statement by Elder Alexander B. Morrison, describing the pioneers:

They were ordinary men and women, plain spoken, hard working, but made noble because they shared a vision, a vision of a different world, a world where injustice and oppression, poverty and ignorance would be dispelled and a world where men and women would be brothers and sisters (*Church News,* 14 Oct. 1995, p. 4).

Discuss the question: How do members of our family work toward that vision today?

E. Have a "pioneer-style" dinner with foods typical of pioneer times. (If you have ancestors who crossed the plains, see if any of your relatives have preserved family recipes from that period.) Alternatively, serve dishes typical of the country from which your ancestors came.

F. If applicable, recount the history of how your ancestors came to settle in this country. Why did they leave their homes? What challenges did they face during the journey, or after they arrived?

G. As a family, research the history of your community's pioneers (first settlers). How did your community come to be? What different religious or ethnic groups have contributed to your community?

H. Make a trip to a site that forms part of your family or community heritage. This might be a Church historical site, a place that plays a significant role in your family history, or something as close to home as the local town hall.

I. In the spirit of remembering or preserving your family's heritage, carry out an activity related to family history: writing personal histories, preserving memorabilia, working on scrapbooks or books of remembrance, looking at old family albums, preparing the names of ancestors for temple work, and so on.

Coming Forth of the Book of Mormon
(September 21)

Note: September 21 is the date of Joseph's visitation by the angel Moroni. An alternative date to commemorate the coming forth of the Book of Mormon would be March 26, when the first printed copies were made available to the public.

Songs and Hymns

Easter Hosanna (*Children's Songbook* 68)
This Is My Beloved Son (*Children's Songbook* 76)
An Angel Came to Joseph Smith (*Children's Songbook* 86)
The Golden Plates (*Children's Songbook* 86)
Book of Mormon Stories (*Children's Songbook* 118)
An Angel from on High (*Hymns* 13)
What Glorious Scenes Mine Eyes Behold (*Hymns* 16)

Lesson Ideas
A. Another Testament of Jesus Christ
Book of Mormon Title Page (To the convincing of all that Jesus is the Christ.)

2 Nephi 25:23, 26 (We write to persuade our brethren to believe in Christ.)

D&C 3:19-20 (That they may rely upon the merits of Jesus Christ.)

- How does the Book of Mormon bear witness of Jesus Christ?
- How does the Book of Mormon teach us to rely on Christ's merits?
- How has the Book of Mormon brought our family closer to the Savior?

B. The Keystone of Our Religion

Book of Mormon Introduction, paragraph 6 (The keystone of our religion.)

D&C 42:12 (Ye shall teach from the Book of Mormon.)

Aritcles of Faith 1:8 (We believe the Book of Mormon to be the word of God.)

- What does it mean to say that the Book of Mormon is the keystone of our religion?
- What role does the Book of Mormon play in our family's spirituality?
- How have the Book of Mormon's teachings brought us closer to God?

C. God Speaks to All Nations

Book of Mormon Title Page (The Eternal God manifests himself to all nations.)

1 Nephi 13:41 (One God and one Shepherd over all the earth.)

2 Nephi 29:7-8, 11 (I command all peoples to write the words I speak unto them.)

- How is the Book of Mormon a sign that God reveals himself to all peoples?
- Why will every people be judged by their own books (see 2 Nephi 29:11)?
- How has our family's faith been strengthened by other nations' testimonies?

D. God Speaks Today

2 Nephi 29:8-9 (I have spoken one word; I can speak another.)

Moroni 7:35-37 (These things show that angels have not ceased to appear.)

D&C 20:5-12 (God inspires men in this age as in generations of old.)

• How does the Book of Mormon attest that revelation is on-going?

• Why is God's will revealed only gradually?

• How have members of our family experienced personal revela-tion?

E. The Fulfilment of God's Promises

2 Nephi 29:1-2 (That I may remember the promises which I have made.)

3 Nephi 21:2, 7 (A sign that the work of the Father hath com-menced.)

JS-H 1:34-41 (Moroni declared that many prophesies were about to be fulfilled.)

• What promises has God made to the peoples of the world?

• How is the Book of Mormon a sign that God will fulfil those promises?

• What is the connection between the coming forth of the Book of Mormon and the fulfilment of the prophesies quoted by Moroni?

Discussions and Activities

A. Read the story of Moroni's visitations to Joseph Smith (JS-H 1:28-54). Invite family members to share their thoughts about the story. What significance does this story have for them?

B. Ask each family member to share a favorite story or passage from the Book of Mormon and to explain why that passage is mean-ingful to them.

C. Read Moroni's promise (Moroni 10:3-5). Emphasize that a tes-timony of the Book of Mormon develops over the course of our entire lives. Invite family members to share experiences that have contributed to their testimonies of the Book of Mormon. These might include:

• Feeling peaceful or calm while reading the Book of Mormon.

• Feeling consoled by words from the Book of Mormon.

• Feeling nourished or replenished by Book of Mormon reading.

• Being guided in a difficult decision by a Book of Mormon pas-sage.

• Applying teachings of the Book of Mormon to your life.

• Striving to follow the example of a figure from the Book of Mormon.

• Being motivated by a Book of Mormon passage to be more Christlike.

• Being reminded by a Book of Mormon passage of God's love for you.

D. Ask each family member to come to the devotional having identified at least one passage from the Book of Mormon which invites people to come to Christ. Discuss the question: In what ways does our family respond to this invitation?

E. Read D&C 10:46-47, 52. Assign each family member to research the beliefs or practices of a different faith. Have each person explain to the rest of the family how teachings from the Book of Mormon reinforce or build on values imparted by that faith.

F. Invite family members to write out their testimonies and place them in copies of the Book of Mormon, for the missionaries to use.

Revelation on the Priesthood
(September 30)

Note: September 30 is the date on which Official Declaration-2 was formally accepted as revelation by the membership of the Church. An alternative date for commemorating this revelation would be June 8, when Official Declaration-2 was first issued.

Songs and Hymns

Children All Over the World (*Children's Songbook* 16)
We Are Different (*Children's Songbook* 263)
Behold, the Mountain of the Lord (*Hymns* 54)
Hark, All Ye Nations! (*Hymns* 264)
Arise, O God, and Shine (*Hymns* 265)
I Am a Child of God (*Hymns* 301, *Children's Songbook* 2)

Lesson Ideas
A. Every Nation, Kindred, and People
Isaiah 56:6-7 (A house of prayer for all people.)

1 Nephi 19:17 (Every nation, kindred, and people shall be blessed.)

D&C 77:11 (Ordained out of every nation, kindred, and people.)

• How did Official Declaration-2 open the way for all peoples to receive the blessings of the gospel?

• How did it help fulfil the prophecy that the temple would be for all people?

• How did it make possible the fulfilment of the prophecy that high priests would be ordained out of every people?

B. All Are Alike Unto God

Galatians 3:26-29 (Ye are all the children of God.)

2 Nephi 26:33 (Black and white—all are alike unto God.)

4 Nephi 1:17 (Neither were there any manner of -ites.)

• How does Official Declaration-2 affirm the truth that all are alike unto God?

• What examples do we see in today's world of racial or ethnic prejudice?

• What can our family do to promote equality among all peoples?

Discussions and Activities

A. Read Official Declaration 2 in its entirety. Invite family members to share their thoughts and feelings about the document.

B. If members of your family remember hearing the revelation announced in 1978, ask them to recount their experience. How did they feel when they heard the announcement?

C. Read Helvecio Martins' interview in the *Friend*, Jan. 1992, pp. 6-7, or Robert Stevenson's story in the *Ensign*, Feb. 1992, pp. 38-39. Invite family members to reflect on how they would have reacted in the same circumstances. Why did black members embrace the Church, despite not being able to receive all the blessings of the priesthood? How must President Kimball have felt about the situation in which these members found themselves? (Reread the second paragraph of Official Declaration-2, which begins, "Aware of the promises . . .")

D. Read the paragraph which introduces Official Declaration-2, in which N. Eldon Tanner explains how the revelation on the priesthood was received. (The paragraph begins, "In early June of this year . . .") Point out that this revelation does not take the form of a document beginning, "Thus saith the Lord." What does this teach us about how revelation works in the restored church?

E. You may have a family member who served a mission in a place (or among a population) which was opened to the work because of Official Declaration-2. If so, ask your family member to describe how the restored gospel has blessed the lives of people there.

F. As part of the closing prayer, pray for peace, understanding, and equality among people of different races and ethnicities.

Honoring Family Members

Mother's Day

Songs and Hymns

Songs about mothers are found in the *Children's Songbook* 202-207. In addition, the following may be appropriate:

O My Father (*Hymns* 292)

Love at Home (*Hymns* 294)

Home Can Be a Heaven on Earth (*Hymns* 298)

Families Can Be Together Forever (*Hymns* 300, *Children's Songbook* 188)

Teach Me to Walk in the Light (*Hymns* 304, *Children's Songbook* 177)

Lesson Ideas

A. Honor Thy Mother

Exodus 20:12 or *Ephesians 6:2-3* or *Mosiah 13:20* (Honor thy mother.)

Proverbs 31:28 (Her children rise up and call her blessed.)

• What is the value of setting aside a day to honor mothers?

• What sacrifices has our family member made for her children?

• More than expressing "appreciation" for our family member on Mother's Day, what can we do in the spirit of rising up and calling her "blessed"?

B. Becoming More Like Our Heavenly Parents

Isaiah 66:13 (God's love is compared to a mother's love.)

D&C 132:19-20 (A continuation of the seeds forever and ever.)

Abraham 4:26-27 (The Gods made human beings in their image.)

• What connection exists between motherhood and exaltation?

• How does a mother participate with the Gods in the work of creation?

• How has motherhood helped our family member learn to love the way God loves?

C. Creating an Eternal Family

Deuteronomy 6:4-7 (Love the Lord thy God; teach these words to thy children.)

D&C 93:38-40 (Bring up your children in light and truth.)

D&C 130:2 (That same sociality which exists here will exist there.)

• How does our family member teach her children to love God?

• How has she helped create family traditions that bring Christ's light into her home?

• How does she help make her family one which its members would want to be part of forever?

D. A Spiritual Guide for Her Children

2 Timothy 1:3-5 (Timothy received his faith from his mother.)

Alma 56:47-48 (The Ammonite youth were taught by their mothers.)

JS-H 1:20 (Joseph Smith's mother was his spiritual confidant.)

• How does our family member set an example of faith for her children?

• How has she tried to teach her children to put their trust in God?

• How does she serve as a spiritual confidant or guide for her children?

E. Rejoicing in Motherhood

Psalms 127:3 (Children are a gift from the Lord.)

Proverbs 23:25 (She that bare thee shall rejoice.)

Moses 5:11 (Despite hardship, Eve rejoiced that she could have seed.)

• How has motherhood been both taxing and rewarding for our family member?

• In what ways does she feel that each of her children is a gift?

• When has she felt the most joy as a mother?

F. Letting Go

Genesis 2:24 (A man shall leave his father and mother.)

Genesis 3:22-23 (Our heavenly parents sent their children into the world.)

D&C 58:28 (They are agents unto themselves.)

• How does our family member feel about seeing her children go their own ways?

• How must our heavenly parents have felt, sending their children into the world to make their own choices?

• How has our family member helped her children learn to exercise their agency?

Discussions and Activities

A. Read Deuteronomy 5:16 or Ephesians 6:2-3. Discuss the questions: What does it mean to "honor" our parents? How is it that honoring our parents helps things to "go well" with us? What wisdom or experience can parents offer their children? To what extent do children have to find their own way through life?

B. Invite family members to express their feelings about their mothers, perhaps in the form of a letter.

C. Ask the family member being honored to describe her relationship with her own mother, growing up. In what ways was the relationship positive? In what ways does she wish the relationship had been different? How did her experience as a daughter shape her ideas about how to be a mother?

D. Invite family members to reflect in their journals on the following questions: How would I sum up my relationship with my mother at this point in my life? What can I do in the coming year to deepen the relationship? (A mother could similarly reflect on her relationships with her children.)

E. If a family member's mother has passed away, take the opportunity to visit her grave, or to hold a brief devotional in her memory. (See "Ideas for a Memorial," in the section of this book titled "Death of a Family Member.") On Mother's Day, it is traditional to wear a white carnation in memory of a mother who has died.

F. As a family, research the origins of Mother's Day. Discuss the questions: What was the original spirit of the holiday? How well is that spirit reflected in our family's Mother's Day observance?

G. Observe Mother's Day by carrying out a special service project, or making a financial contribution, to help needy mothers.

H. Before offering the closing prayer, ask your family member what prayers she feels in need of as a mother.

I. Consider concluding your family's Mother's Day devotional with a priesthood blessing for the family member being honored, in lieu of a closing prayer.

Father's Day

Songs and Hymns

Daddy's Homecoming (*Children's Songbook* 210)
My Dad (*Children's Songbook* 211)
O My Father (*Hymns* 292)
Love at Home (*Hymns* 294)
Home Can Be a Heaven on Earth (*Hymns* 298)
Families Can Be Together Forever (*Hymns* 300, *Children's Songbook* 188)
Teach Me to Walk in the Light (*Hymns* 304, *Children's Songbook* 177)

Lesson Ideas

A. Honor Thy Father

Exodus 20:12 or *Ephesians 6:2-3* or *Mosiah 13:20* (Honor thy father.)

D&C 107:53-54 (Adam's posterity gathered to honor him.)

• What is the value of setting aside a day to honor fathers?

• What sacrifices has our family member made for his children?

• More than expressing "appreciation" for our family member on Father's Day, what can we do in the spirit of rising up and "blessing" him (D&C 107:54)?

B. Becoming More Like Our Heavenly Father

Psalms 103:13 (God's love is compared to a father's love.)

D&C 132:19-20 (A continuation of the seeds forever and ever.)

Abraham 4:26-27 (The Gods made human beings in their image.)

• What connection exists between fatherhood and exaltation?

• How does a father participate with the Gods in the work of creation?

• How has fatherhood helped our family member learn to love the way God loves?

C. Creating an Eternal Family

Deuteronomy 6:4-7 (Love the Lord thy God; teach these words to thy children.)

D&C 93:38-40 (Bring up your children in light and truth.)

D&C 130:2 (That same sociality which exists here will exist there.)

- How does our family member teach his children to love God?
- How has he helped create family traditions that bring Christ's light into his home?
- How does he help make his family one which its members would want to be part of forever?

D. A Spiritual Guide for His Children

1 Thessalonians 1:10-12 (We exhorted and comforted you like a father.)

Enos 1:1 (Enos' father taught him in the nurture of the Lord.)

JS-H 1:48-50 (Joseph Smith's father was his spiritual confidant.)

- What does it mean for a father to teach his children in the nurture of the Lord?
- In what ways does our family member exhort and comfort his children?
- How does he serve as a spiritual confidant or guide for his children?

E. Rejoicing in Fatherhood

Psalms 127:3 (Children are a gift from the Lord.)

Proverbs 23:24 (He that begetteth a wise child shall have joy of him.)

2 Nephi 2:22-23 (Adam accepted hardship in order to have children.)

- How has fatherhood been both taxing and rewarding for our family member?
- In what ways does he feel that each of his children is a gift?
- When has he felt most joy as a father?

F. Letting Go

Genesis 2:24 (A man shall leave his father and mother.)

Genesis 3:22-23 (Heavenly Father sent his children into the world.)

D&C 58:28 (They are agents unto themselves.)

• How does our family member feel about seeing his children go their own ways?

• How must our Heavenly Father have felt, sending his children into the world to make their own choices?

• How has our family member helped his children learn to exercise their agency?

Discussions and Activities

A. Read Deuteronomy 5:16 or Ephesians 6:2-3. Discuss the questions: What does it mean to "honor" our parents? How is it that honoring our parents helps things to "go well" with us? What wisdom or experience can parents offer their children? To what extent do children have to find their own way through life?

B. Invite family members to express their feelings about their fathers, perhaps in the form of a letter.

C. Ask the family member being honored to describe his relationship with his own father, growing up. In what ways was the relationship positive? In what ways does he wish the relationship had been different? How did his experience as a son shape his ideas about how to be a father?

D. Invite family members to reflect in their journals on the following questions: How would I sum up my relationship with my father at this point in my life? What can I do in the coming year to deepen the relationship? (A father could similarly reflect on his relationships with his children.)

E. If a family member's father has passed away, take the opportunity to visit his grave, or to hold a brief devotional in his memory. (See "Ideas for a Memorial," in the section of this book titled "Death of a Family Member.")

F. Before offering the closing prayer, ask your family member what prayers he feels in need of as a father.

G. Consider concluding your family's Fathers Day devotional with a priesthood blessing for the family member being honored. He might receive this blessing from his father, or from a son who holds the Melchizedek priesthood.

Birthdays

Songs and Hymns

Birthday songs are found in the *Children's Songbook,* pp. 282-285. In addition, the following may be appropriate:

I'm Thankful to Be Me (*Children's Songbook* 11)
Heavenly Father, Now I Pray (*Children's Songbook* 19)
For Thy Bounteous Blessings (*Children's Songbook* 21)
I Will Follow God's Plan (*Children's Songbook* 164)
Now Thank We All Our God (*Hymns* 95)
Come, Let Us Anew (*Hymns* 217)
I Am a Child of God (*Hymns* 301, *Children's Songbook* 2)

Lesson Ideas

A. Thanks for Another Year

Psalms 105:1-2 (Give thanks unto the Lord; talk of all his wondrous works.)

2 Corinthians 9:15 (Thanks be unto God for his unspeakable gift.)

Mosiah 2:20-21 (God has kept and preserved you.)

• How has God blessed our family member during the past year?
• What difference does it make to know that our lives are a gift?
• How can we make this birthday celebration an act of thanksgiving?

B. Wishes for the Coming Year

Psalms 37:3-5 (The Lord shall give thee the desires of thine heart.)

2 Nephi 32:9 (Pray that the Lord shall consecrate thy performance.)

D&C 6:8 (You shall be the means of doing much good.)

• What does our family member hope to achieve in the coming year?
• What chances will he/she have to do good in the coming year?
• What "birthday wishes" might our family member ask of God?

C. Growing in Grace

Matthew 5:48 or *3 Nephi 12:48* (Be ye perfect.)

D&C 50:40 (Ye are little children; ye must grow in grace.)

D&C 93:11-14 (The Son continued from grace to grace.)

- Why is spiritual growth a life-long process?
- How do we open ourselves up to the grace we need to grow spiritually?
- How has our family member grown spiritually since his/her last birthday?

D. Honoring Our Family Member

Of the scriptures marked with an asterisk (*), choose the one that is most appropriate to the situation.

*Psalms 127:3 (Children are a gift from the Lord.)

*Exodus 20:12 or *Mosiah 13:20* (Honor thy father and thy mother.)

*Leviticus 19:32 (Honor the elderly.)

John 13:34 (Love one another as I have loved you.)

Mosiah 2:18 (Labor to serve one another.)

- Why do we honor one another on our birthdays?
- How has our family been blessed by the person whose birthday we are celebrating?
- How can we express our love to that person on his/her birthday?

Discussions and Activities

A. Open the devotional (or birthday celebration) with a prayer, thanking God for the gift of your family member and for bringing your family member safe through another year.

B. Ask family members to make homemade birthday cards. Each card could depict either something accomplished in the past year by the person whose birthday is being celebrated, or a wish on behalf of that person for the coming year.

C. Go around the room, giving each person a chance to wish your family member a happy birthday and to congratulate him/her on some accomplishment of the past year.

D. Before your family member makes his/her birthday wishes and blows out the candles, ask everyone else in the family to voice a hope or wish of their own on behalf of the person.

E. Ask each person in the family to "give" an act of service to the person whose birthday is being celebrated.

F. Before opening birthday presents, read Matthew 7:9-11 or 3 Nephi 14:9-11. Discuss the question: Why do we give gifts to one another on our birthdays?

G. Conclude the devotional (or birthday celebration) with a prayer, asking God to keep your family member safe during the coming year and to grant him/her the desires of his/her heart.

Wedding Anniversaries

Songs and Hymns
Where Love Is (*Children's Songbook* 138)
Love Is Spoken Here (*Children's Songbook* 190)
The Wise Man and the Foolish Man (*Children's Songbook* 281)
Let Us Oft Speak Kind Words (*Hymns* 232)
Love at Home (*Hymns* 294)
Home Can Be a Heaven on Earth (*Hymns* 298)
Families Can Be Together Forever (*Hymns* 300, *Children's Songbook* 188)

Lesson Ideas
A. Becoming One Flesh
Genesis 2:18-24 or *Moses 3:18-24* or *Abraham 5:14-18* (They shall be one flesh.)

1 Corinthians 7:3-4 (Husband and wife give themselves to one another.)

Mosiah 18:21 (Hearts knit together in love.)

• What challenges have arisen in the couple's relationship over the last year?

• In what ways does the couple feel that they have grown closer in the last year?

• What common goals will they work for in the coming year?

B. Supporting One Another
Ecclesiastes 4:9-12 (Two are better than one.)

Philippians. 2:1-4 (Look to the other's welfare.)

Mosiah 2:17-18 (Labor to serve one another.)
- How has the couple supported one another over the last year?
- In what ways have they served one another?
- How do the couple make themselves aware of each other's needs?

C. Growing in Charity

Matthew 7:24-27 or *3 Nephi 14:24-27* (Build your house upon the rock.)

Colossians 3:12-15 (Put on charity, the bond of perfectness.)

Moroni 7:45-48 (Moroni exhorts us to pray for charity.)

- What is the difference between a marriage built on charity, and one built on romance, child-rearing, financial ties, or a need for stability?
- How have we seen this couple show charity for one another during the past year?
- Why do we need to pray for charity?

D. Supping with the Savior

Matthew 18:19-20 (Where two gather in my name, I am in their midst.)

Revelation 3:20 (Jesus will sup with those who open their door to him.)

D&C 88:63 (Draw near unto me and I will draw near unto you.)

- What traditions have the couple established to invite the Savior into their home?
- In what ways have the couple sensed God's presence in their marriage?
- How has the gospel helped the couple draw closer to one another?

E. Building an Eternal Marriage

D&C 132:19-20 (The new and everlasting covenant of marriage.)

D&C 130:2 (That same sociality which exists here will exist there.)

D&C 90:24 (All things shall work for good if you remember the covenant.)

- As the couple has worked through difficulties, what difference has it made to know that their marriage has been sealed?

- What aspects of their present relationship would the couple like to last forever?
- How would the couple like to see their relationship improve?

Discussions and Activities

A. As a couple, read to one another selections from the journal entries you each wrote during the period when you were engaged or newly married. Discuss together the questions:

- In what ways have our expectations of this marriage been met?
- In what ways have our expectations matured?
- How has our relationship developed over time?
- Have we lost something in our relationship that we would like to recover?
- Have we lost something that has been replaced with something better?

B. Review the promises you made to your spouse when you were married. Reflect in your journal on the question: How well am I keeping those promises?

C. The couple might find it meaningful to verbally renew the promises they made to one another when they began their married life.

D. If other family members are participating in the anniversary celebration, invite them to share their observations of how the couple has grown in their life together. Invite the couple to comment on what they have learned in the course of the past year about making marriage work.

E. Give family members an opportunity to voice their continuing best wishes and hopes on behalf of the couple.

F. Invite adolescents to reflect in their journals on the question: What have I learned from observing my parents (or older siblings, etc.) about the kind of marriage I want to have when that time comes?

G. Before retiring to bed on their anniversary night, the couple might consider offering not one, but two prayers—one voiced by each of them. In his/her prayer, each member of the couple could thank God for the other and pray on the other's behalf.

Reflecting on Citizenship and Stewardship

Martin Luther King's Birthday
(Human Rights Day)

Songs and Hymns
Children All Over the World (*Children's Songbook* 16)
Dare to Do Right (*Children's Songbook* 158)
We Are Different (*Children's Songbook* 263)
I Am a Child of God (*Hymns* 301, *Children's Songbook* 2)
America the Beautiful (*Hymns* 338)
My Country, 'Tis of Thee (*Hymns* 339)

Lesson Ideas
A. All Are Alike Unto God
Galatians 3:26-29 (Ye are all the children of God.)
2 Nephi26:33 (Black and white—all are alike unto God.)
4 Nephi 1:17 (Neither were there any manner of -ites.)
   • How did Martin Luther King affirm the truth that all are alike unto God?
   • What examples do we see in the world today of racial or ethnic prejudice?
   • How do Latter-day Saints promote equality among all peoples?

B. Liberty and Justice for All
Micah 6:8 (What doth the Lord require of thee but to do justly?)
Mosiah 29:32 (I desire that this inequality should be no more.)
D&C 98:5-7 (Constitutional law should protect the rights of all.)
   • How does the Constitution provide liberty and justice for all?
   • In what ways, historically, has our country fallen short of that ideal?
   • How can our family stand up for equality and justice?

C. Preserving Human Rights

Psalms 10:17-18 (God will cause that there be no more oppression.)

D&C 134:2 (Governments must hold certain rights inviolate.)

Moses 6:43 (Ye are my brethren.)

• Where in today's world do we see the rights listed in D&C 134:2 being violated?

• What difference would it make if people treated each other as God's children?

• Whom could we name as examples of people who have defended human rights?

Discussions and Activities

A. As a family, compile a list of as many different racial or ethnic groups as you can think of who currently live in the United States. Discuss the questions: How is our country blessed by this diversity? What challenges does it create? Psalms 133 could provide a scriptural basis for this discussion.

B. Ask each family member to come to the devotional with a newspaper or magazine article which shows how race relations continue to be a source of conflict in American society. Discuss the question: What can our family do to promote harmony between different racial groups?

C. Pick a regime somewhere in the world, past or present, known for human rights violations. As a family, research that regime's history. How did (or does) the regime justify its actions? How do people reach a point where they are willing to violate others' human rights?

D. Mark on a world map places where racial or ethnic conflicts, or human rights violations, are occurring today. Then read Moses 7:24-26 and Ether 8:26. Discuss the question: What will it take to bring an end to the violence in these parts of the world?

E. In the spirit of D&C 93:53, assign family members to prepare presentations on different people or events from the civil rights movement. (Topics might include Little Rock, Rosa Parks, James Meredith, or Martin Luther King, Jr.) As you discuss each other's presentations, focus on the question: What can we learn from these individuals' examples about finding the courage to stand up for what we know is right?

F. Read Martin Luther King's "I Have a Dream" speech. Note the quotation from Isaiah 40:4. Discuss the questions: How well has King's dream been realized in our nation? In our world?

G. As a family, make a contribution of time or money to an organization that works to promote or defend human rights.

H. As part of the closing prayer, pray for peace, understanding, and equality among people of different races and ethnicities. Make mention in your prayer of specific parts of the world where human rights violations occur.

Presidents' Day

Songs and Hymns

The Twelfth Article of Faith (*Children's Songbook* 131)
O God, Our Help in Ages Past (*Hymns* 31)
Battle Hymn of the Republic (*Hymns* 60)
God of Our Fathers, Whose Almighty Hand (*Hymns* 78)
America the Beautiful (*Hymns* 338)

Lesson Ideas

A. George Washington, Father of His Country

1 Nephi 13:16-19 (Nephi foresaw the American colonists winning independence.)

3 Nephi 21:4 (Jesus prophesied the American settlers would be a free people.)

D&C 101:80 (God raised up wise men to establish the Constitution.)

• What was George Washington's role in the fight for American independence?

• What was his role in establishing this country's constitutional government?

• How have independence and constitutional government been a blessing for the people of this country?

B. Abraham Lincoln, the Great Emancipator

Leviticus 26:13 (I have broken the bands of your yoke.)

Mosiah 2:13 (King Benjamin forbade slavery.)

D&C 101:79-80 (No one should be in bondage to another.)

• In what sense could Abraham Lincoln be called an instrument of God?

• Why did King Benjamin class slavery as a kind of "wickedness"?

• Why was slavery an accepted institution for so long?

C. Rule by the People

Mosiah 29:26 (Do your business by the voice of the people.)

Alma 27:20-22 (The voice of the people regarding the Anti-Nephi-Lehies.)

Helaman 1:1-5 (Nephite leaders chosen by the voice of the people.)

• What arguments might be made against choosing our leaders by popular vote?

• Why is our country willing to trust the judgment of the majority in this matter?

• What responsibilities does rule by an elected president lay on us, the citizens?

D. Electing Wise Leaders

D&C 98:8-10 (Seek for honest and wise leaders.)

D&C 134:3 (Seek for leaders who will administer equity and justice.)

• Which presidents do you consider examples of honesty, wisdom, or goodness?

• In what ways have past presidents administered equity and justice?

• As citizens, how can we educate ourselves about presidential candidates?

Discussions and Activities

A. Open the devotional with prayer, thanking God for the freedom to choose our country's leaders. Pray that we will exercise that freedom wisely and responsibly. You might also deem it appropriate to thank Heavenly Father for particular presidents whose administrations you feel served the country well.

B. Invite each family member to make a brief presentation on a past president he/she admires. Why does your family member feel this president served as a good ruler or a good role model?

C. As a family, research the lives of Washington or Lincoln in order to gain a greater appreciation for these individuals. Questions to focus on might include:

- What were their personalities like?
- What were their family lives like?
- What struggles or personal tragedies did they face?
- Why did they decide to pursue politics?
- What were they criticized for?
- How were they able to accomplish what they did?
- How were they aided or supported by others?

D. In the course of this devotional (particularly if the lesson, "Electing Wise Leaders," is used), it may become evident that family members have differing political views. Read D&C 38:27 and discuss the questions: Why do people tend to have strong feelings about their political differences? As a family and as a country, how can we preserve a sense of unity despite political differences?

E. Read Article of Faith 12. Point out that a presidential election generally leaves a sizable portion of the country disappointed at the results. Discuss the question: How should we respond to the administration of a president to whom we are politically opposed?

F. Read 1 Timothy 2:1-3. Resolve to pray regularly for the president as a family, if you don't already. If your family is opposed to the current president, or if family members are divided in their feelings toward the current president, discuss what could be said in a prayer on behalf of the president that would be heartfelt and would reflect the feelings of all family members. Matthew 5:44-45 (3 Nephi 12:44-45) or D&C 27:18 could provide a scriptural basis for this discussion.

Arbor Day or Earth Day

Songs and Hymns

A Song of Thanks (*Children's Songbook* 20)
My Heavenly Father Loves Me (*Children's Songbook* 228)
All Things Bright and Beautiful (*Children's Songbook* 231)
The World Is So Big (*Children's Songbook* 235)
All Creatures of Our God and King (*Hymns* 62)
How Great Thou Art (*Hymns* 86)
God Is Love (*Hymns* 87)
For the Beauty of the Earth (*Hymns* 92)
We Give Thee But Thine Own (*Hymns* 218)

Lesson Ideas

A. The Gift of Trees

Genesis 1:11-12 or *Moses 2:11-12* or *Abraham 4:11-12* (God created trees.)

Helaman 2:9 (The Nephites cultivated trees.)

D&C 59:17-18 (Trees are made for our benefit and use.)

- In what ways do trees benefit us?
- How can we show wisdom in our use of trees?
- How can we show thanks to God for the gift of trees?

B. Trees as Spiritual Types

Matthew 13:31-32 (The kingdom of heaven is like a tree.)

Revelation 22:1-2 (John saw the tree of life in the celestial city.)

1 Nephi 8:10-12 (Lehi saw the tree of life in his dream.)

Alma 32:28, 37, 42 (Alma compared God's word to a tree.)

D&C 97:8-9 (I will cause them to bring forth as a fruitful tree.)

- Why is a tree an especially appropriate symbol of God's love?
- Why are God's kingdom and word compared to trees?
- How have we seen members of our family "bring forth as a fruitful tree"?

C. Stewards of the Earth

Genesis 1:26-28 or *Moses 2:26-28* or *Abraham 4:26-28* (Let them have dominion.)

Luke 16:1-2 (The parable of the wasteful steward.)

D&C 59:18-20 (These things were made to be used with judgment.)

- What does it mean to be a steward?
- What examples do we see of unwise stewardship of the earth?
- How can our family promote wiser use of the earth's resources?

D. Renewing the Earth

Isaiah 51:3 or *2 Nephi 8:3* (He will make her wilderness like Eden.)

Isaiah 61:4 (They shall raise up the former desolations.)

D&C 133:29 (The parched ground shall no longer be a thirsty land.)

- Where do we see desolation and waste in today's world?
- What efforts are being made to repair these desolations?
- How might our family contribute to these efforts?

E. Praying with Creation

Moses 7:48 (Wo is me, the mother of men.)

Romans 8:22 (The whole creation travaileth in pain.)

Revelation 5:11-13 (John saw all creation praising God.)

D&C 128:23 (Let the eternal creations declare his name forever!)

- How do human beings cause creation to suffer?
- If we could hear creation praying, what do we imagine it would say?
- What difference does it make to imagine all creation worshiping with us?

Discussions and Activities

A. Research the origins of Arbor Day or Earth Day. Discuss the question: How does the founder of this holiday exemplify being anxiously engaged in a good cause (D&C 58:26-28)?

B. As part of the lesson "Trees as Spiritual Types," have each family member create a drawing of a favorite tree. Invite each person to label his/her drawing with a slogan taken from one of the scriptures used in the lesson.

C. As a family, create a drawing or collage depicting Revelation 5:11-13 or D&C 128:23. Depict your own family in the drawing or collage as well.

D. Read Psalms 104 in its entirety. Ask family members to describe things in creation that have caused them to feel awe, or which have made them aware of God's love.

E. Read D&C 1:17-18. Discuss the questions: What does "calamity" mean? What do we see happening to the earth and its resources that could be considered calamitous? What principles taught by the modern prophets could help the peoples of the world avoid environmental disaster?

F. Read D&C 5:5, 19. Point out that the word "repent" means not only seeking forgiveness for sin, but also changing the way one lives. Discuss the question: What changes do the inhabitants of the earth need to make in the way we live in order to prevent famine, disease, and the destruction of natural resources?

G. Celebrate Arbor Day by planting a tree. If a family member has died in the past year, plant the tree in that person's memory.

H. Participate in a community activity, or go to an informational exhibit, held in connection with Arbor Day or Earth Day. If there are no such activities or exhibits in your area, consider organizing one yourselves, even if just on a small scale.

I. Make a contribution of time or money to an organization that promotes reforestation or some other conservation-minded activity.

J. As a family, resolve to make specific changes in your lifestyle for the good of the environment or in the interest of conservation.

K. In the closing prayer, make mention of specific environmental concerns our world faces today.

Memorial Day

Songs and Hymns
Truth from Elijah (*Children's Songbook* 90)
The Hearts of the Children (*Children's Songbook* 92)

I Have a Family Tree (*Children's Songbook* 199)
O God, Our Help in Ages Past (*Hymns* 31)
Each Life That Touches Ours for Good (*Hymns* 293)
America the Beautiful (*Hymns* 338)
The Star-Spangled Banner (*Hymns* 340)

Lesson Ideas

A. Days of Memorial

Exodus 12:12-14 (Passover was a day of memorial.)
Joshua 4:5-7 (Joshua established a memorial.)
Esther 9:24-28 (Purim was a memorial.)
Alma 62:48-50 (The Nephites remembered God's aid.)

- What do these passages teach us about the purpose of memorials?
- What are we meant to remember on Memorial Day?
- How can we make our family's Memorial Day observance an act of thanksgiving?

B. Honoring the Dead

Genesis 35:19-20 (Jacob set a pillar on Rachel's grave.)
Genesis 50:4-5 (Joseph honored Jacob's wishes about his burial.)
Mark 16:1-2 (The women came to anoint Jesus' body.)
John 20:1-2 (The disciples were upset to think Jesus' body had been taken.)

- How do we honor the dead in our own culture and time?
- Why does it matter so much to us where and how deceased people's bodies are cared for?
- Why do we pay such attention to marking and caring for graves?

C. Remembering the Fallen

Isaiah 3:25-26 or *2 Nephi 13:25-26* (Thy men shall fall by the sword.)
Jeremiah 31:15 or *Matthew 2:18* (Rachel weeping for her children.)
Alma 28:4-6 (The Nephites mourned for the slain.)

- In what sense is Memorial Day a time of mourning?
- What was accomplished by the death of so many people?
- How can we, the living, ensure that these deaths are not in vain?

D. Remembering Our Ancestors

Deuteronomy 32:7 (Remember the days of old.)

Ether 6:30 (Orihah remembered what the Lord did for his forebears.)

Malachi 4:5-6 or *3 Nephi 25:5-6* (The hearts of the children.)

- How has God blessed our ancestors?
- What difference does that knowledge make in our own lives?
- How does Memorial Day turn our hearts to our forebears?

E. A Family Reunion

Genesis 25:8-10 (Abraham died and was gathered to his people.)

Luke 20:38 (He is not a God of the dead; all live unto him.)

D&C 130:2 (That same sociality which exists here will exist there.)

- In what sense is death a family reunion for the one who dies?
- In what sense is a visit to a loved one's grave a family reunion reaching across the veil?
- In what sense could it be said that we and our dead have never been separated?

Discussions and Activities

A. Read and discuss John McCrae's famous memorial poem, "In Flanders Field." You might also be interested in reading from the war poems of Siegfried Sassoon and Wilfred Owen, who, like McCrae, wrote out of their experiences as soldiers during World War I.

B. Make a list of wars and conflicts in American history. Find out how many people died in each of these conflicts. (Include, if figures are available, the dead from both sides of each conflict.) Add up the total. Calculate how long it would take to observe a minute of silence for each individual who died. Then ask family members to observe a minute or two of silence for all of the dead together.

C. If your family has ancestors who died in war, assign family members to recount the stories of these ancestors' lives.

D. Pass around the room some token of remembrance—perhaps a poppy, a tiny flag, or a lighted candle. As each family member receives the token, invite him/her to state something he/she has resolved to do in the spirit of honoring or remembering the dead. (Alternatively, family members could voice thanks for blessings they have received as a result of sacrifices made by the dead.)

E. Make arrangements to help clean up a local cemetery or decorate the graves of soldiers.

F. Plan to visit the graves of loved ones during Memorial Day weekend. If you have relatives in the area, you might make the visit double as a family get-together.

G. This might be an appropriate occasion to discuss the funeral and burial wishes of older family members. D&C 101:72 could set the tone for this discussion ("Let these things be done in their time, but not in haste; and observe to have all things prepared before you").

H. Arrange photographs of deceased relatives on or around the dinner table, as a way of acknowledging that they are still part of the family and thus, in a symbolic sense, are included in your family meal. A picnic near the graves of family members would provide the same kind of experience.

I. Ask each family member to prepare a brief presentation on one of your ancestors. Focus on the questions: In what ways did this ancestor exemplify Christlike living? What sacrifices did this ancestor make that have blessed our family?

J. Carry out an activity related to family history: writing personal histories, preserving memorabilia, working on scrapbooks or books of remembrance, looking at old family albums, preparing the names of ancestors for temple work, and so on.

K. This would be an especially appropriate time to remember family members who have died during the past year. See "Ideas for a Memorial," in the section of this book titled "Death of a Family Member."

Independence Day

Songs and Hymns

Book of Mormon Stories (*Children's Songbook* 118)
My Country (*Children's Songbook* 224)
My Flag, My Flag (*Children's Songbook* 225)
O God, Our Help in Ages Past (*Hymns* 31)
God of Our Fathers, Whose Almighty Hand (*Hymns* 78)
America the Beautiful (*Hymns* 338)

My Country, 'Tis of Thee (*Hymns* 339)
The Star-Spangled Banner (*Hymns* 340)

Lesson Ideas

A. An Independent Nation

1 Nephi 13:16-19 (Nephi foresaw the American colonies would win independence.)

3 Nephi 21:4 (Jesus prophesied the American settlers would be a free people.)

D&C 101:79-80 (It is not right that anyone should be in bondage.)

• Why did the American revolutionaries refuse to go on being colonists?

• Why did the British government reject the colonies' claim to independence?

• Where else in the world have colonies had to fight for their independence?

B. Rule by the People

2 Nephi 10:11-12 (There shall be no kings upon the land.)
Mosiah 23:6-9 (It is not expedient that ye should have a king.)
Mosiah 29:26 (Do your business by the voice of the people.)

• What arguments might be made in favor of rule by an absolute sovereign?

• Why did the Founders insist on a democratic, constitutional government instead?

• What responsibilities does self-government lay on us, the citizens?

C. All Are Created Equal

Acts 10:34 (God is no respecter of persons.)
2 Nephi 26:33 (All are alike unto God.)
D&C 101:76-80 (The rights and protection of all flesh.)

• How have Americans lived out the principle that all people are created equal?

• In what ways, historically, have we fallen short of that ideal?

• How does our family show a commitment to equality for all people?

D. A Shot Heard 'Round the World

Isaiah 58:6 (Let the oppressed go free.)

2 Corinthians 3:17 (Where the Spirit of the Lord is, there is liberty.)

D&C 98:5-7 (Constitutional law belongs to all mankind.)

• How have other nations been inspired by the American experiment?

• In what sense is the rise of democracy worldwide the work of the Spirit?

• How does our family help promote liberty and democracy?

Discussions and Activities

A. Ask each family member to prepare a presentation on someone who played an influential role in the American revolution or in the establishment of constitutional law and civil liberty in the United States. As family members prepare their presentations, invite them to reflect on D&C 101:79-80.

B. Create a Freedom Shrine for your home—that is, a display of documents that embody democratic values. These might include the Declaration of Independence, the Bill of Rights, other foundational documents, statements by political or religious leaders, or passages of scripture.

C. In the spirit of D&C 93:53, assign family members to learn about the governments of different democratic countries around the world. Note the diverse ways these countries apply the principles of democratic rule or constitutional law.

D. Read the Declaration of Independence in its entirety. Ask family members to comment on portions of the Declaration that stand out to them. One question in particular to focus on might be: How does the Constitution, written over 10 years later, reflect the values and concerns expressed in the Declaration?

E. Note that when the Declaration of Independence speaks of God, it uses the term "Creator." Explain that this term was chosen because people from a variety of religious backgrounds could relate to it. Discuss the question: How do Americans today meet the challenge of living in a society where people hold a variety of beliefs about religion?

F. Read or summarize the Bill of Rights. Discuss the question: How did Americans' experiences as colonists lead them to demand the protections enshrined in the Bill of Rights?

G. Celebrate the country's birthday party with a cake and candles. Ask each family member to voice a wish or hope on behalf of the country (or on behalf of liberty and democracy in general). Then blow out the candles together.

H. Obtain a list of the questions about American government and history that people must be prepared to answer when they apply for U.S. citizenship. Create a game that lets family members test their ability to answer the questions.

I. Celebrate Independence Day by carrying out a service project in the spirit of the exhortation: "Ask not what your country can do for you; ask what you can do for your country."

J. Read and discuss the following words of Spencer W. Kimball, written in connection with the U.S. Bicentennial:

We are a warlike people, easily distracted from our assignment of preparing for the coming of the Lord. When enemies rise up, we commit vast resources to the fabrication of gods of stone and steel—ships, planes, missiles, fortifications—and depend on them for protection and deliverance. When threatened, we become anti-enemy instead of pro-kingdom of God; we train a man in the art of war and call him a patriot, thus, in the manner of Satan's counterfeit of true patriotism, perverting the Savior's teaching: "Love your enemies, bless them that curse you, do good to them that hate you, and pray for them which despitefully use you, and persecute you . . ." (*Ensign*, June 1976, p. 6)

K. As a family, create a poster or collage based on D&C 109:54-55.

L. Ask family members to come to the devotional prepared to name specific problems or challenges faced by the United States today. Make mention of these during the closing prayer.

Labor Day

Songs and Hymns
Thank Thee, Father (*Children's Songbook* 24)
When We're Helping (*Children's Songbook* 198)
Softly Now the Light of Day (*Hymns* 160)
I Have Work Enough to Do (*Hymns* 224)
Improve the Shining Moments (*Hymns* 226)
Today, While the Sun Shines (*Hymns* 229)
Put Your Shoulder to the Wheel (*Hymns* 252)

Lesson Ideas
A. Honoring Workers
Psalms 90:17 (Establish thou the work of our hands upon us.)
Ether 10:22-28 (They were exceedingly industrious and prospered.)
• Why do we have a holiday to honor labor?
• How has our country been blessed by the industry of workers?
• How can we make our family's Labor Day observance an act of thanksgiving?

B. A Productive Life
John 5:17 (My Father worketh hitherto, and I work.)
Alma 36:25 (The Lord doth give me joy in the fruit of my labors.)
D&C 58:26-28 (We should be anxiously engaged in a good cause.)
• How does working in a good cause help make our lives meaningful?
• How does it make us more Christlike?
• How do members of our family find joy in the fruits of their labors?

C. A Rest from Labor
Genesis 2:2 or *Moses 3:2* or *Abraham 5:2* (God rested from his labors.)
Exodus 23:10-12 (The Sabbath principle.)

D&C 10:4 (Do not labor more than you have strength.)

• What do we learn from the fact that even God set aside a time for rest?

• In what sense are measures like the 8-hour work day, the 40-hour work week, and legal holidays applications of the Sabbath principle?

• How might we liken D&C 10:4 to our own lives?

D. A New School Year

Daniel 1:17 (God gave them knowledge and skill in all learning.)

2 Peter 1:4-7 (Add to your virtue knowledge.)

D&C 88:118 (Seek learning by study and also by faith.)

• How does schooling help us develop our divine potential?

• How have we seen our family members grow in the course of their schooling?

• How can we seek God's blessings as we begin a new school year?

Discussions and Activities

A. Ask each family member to come to the devotional with at least one scripture related to work or workers. Have family members explain why the scriptures they chose were significant to them. (Alternatively, you could ask family members to come with scriptures related to schooling or education.)

B. Explain that many of the working conditions we take for granted today represent hard-won gains by workers in the past. In the spirit of Deuteronomy 32:7, ask family members to prepare brief presentations on how the following came to be:

• Child labor laws
• The eight-hour work day
• The minimum wage
• Retirement and Social Security
• Workplace safety regulations

C. As a family, make a contribution of time or money to an organization that works for better working conditions or job opportunities (in the developing world, for instance).

D. As a family, discuss each other's talents or special abilities. How might these abilities equip family members for success in certain careers? (In the case of family members who already have careers, you might discuss how they could develop their talents and abilities further.)

E. Meet individually with high school and college-aged family members to discuss their on-going career preparation. What will they do during the coming school year that will better equip them to move into their preferred career? What can other family members do to help or support them?

F. Invite family members to voice their hopes, concerns, or anxieties about the coming school year. Make mention of these in the closing prayer.

G. Consider closing the devotional with a priesthood blessing for each family member who is about to start, or return to, school.

Columbus Day

Songs and Hymns

Book of Mormon Stories (*Children's Songbook* 118)
We Are Different (*Children's Songbook* 263)
Father in Heaven (*Hymns* 133)
Jehovah, Lord of Heaven and Earth (*Hymns* 269)
God Moves in a Mysterious Way (*Hymns* 285)
America the Beautiful (*Hymns* 338)

Lesson Ideas

A. An Event Foretold

Isaiah 46:9-10 (God declares the end from the beginning.)
1 Nephi 13:12 (Nephi foresaw the discovery of the New World.)
D&C 3:1-2 (The purposes of God cannot be frustrated.)

• What difference does it make to know that God sees the end from the beginning?

• What has happened as a result of the discovery of the New World which has furthered God's purposes?

B. Reuniting the Human Family

Acts 17:24-26 (God hath made one of one blood all nations.)
Genesis 10:1-5 (The human family became divided.)

1 *Nephi 13:12* (Nephi foresaw contact between the Old and New Worlds.)

D&C 45:71 (The Saints shall be gathered from all nations.)

• Why has there been so much division within the human family?

• How did the discovery of the New World open up the possibility of bringing together people from all branches of the human family?

• How has the restored church helped create unity among people all over the world?

C. A Land Free to All

1 *Nephi 13:12-13* (The Gentiles went forth out of captivity.)
2 *Nephi 1:5-6* (This land shall be for all whom the Lord brings.)
D&C 10:50-51 (This land might be free unto all.)

• How many different peoples today call the New World home?

• What forces have brought so many peoples together on one continent?

• What challenges does that diversity create?

D. Blossom as the Rose

1 *Nephi 13:13-14* (The Lamanites were smitten by the Gentiles.)
3 *Nephi 20:22, 25* (The powers of heaven will be with the Lamanites.)

D&C 49:24 (The Lamanites shall blossom as the rose.)

• What happened to the native peoples of this continent as a result of the colonization of the New World?

• What promises are made to the native peoples in these passages?

• How have those promises begun to be fulfilled?

Discussions and Activities

A. Read 1 Nephi 13:12. Point out that Columbus believed God was inspiring him to find a new route to the Indies; he had no idea that he was actually going to discover the New World. Discuss the question: What can we learn from Columbus' story about the way we ourselves are guided by the Spirit?

B. As a family, imagine how the world would be different if the discovery of the New World had never occurred. Some questions to research might include:

• How did the people of the Old World benefit from New World foods like the potato?

• How have plants native to the New World been used for medicinal purposes?

• How did the discovery of the New World make possible experiments in democracy?

• How did the discovery of the New World make possible the Restoration?

C. Compile as complete a list as you can of the peoples—both native and immigrant—who have settled in the New World. Read 2 Nephi 1:6. Discuss the question: Why would God will so many different peoples to share one continent?

D. Read 1 Nephi 13:12-13 and discuss the question: What different kinds of captivity did people come to the New World to flee? In what ways were the societies they built in the New World better than those they had left behind? In what ways did they reproduce the problems and mistakes of their old societies?

E. As a family, create a map showing all the nations which make up the Americas, with their respective flags. Label the map "A New World for All of Us" or "We Share a Land of Promise." Discuss the questions: What problems face the American continent today? How do the countries of the Americas work together for the common good of their peoples?

F. Recount your own family's history in the New World. How long have your ancestors been on this continent? What brought them here? What struggles did they face in establishing themselves here?

G. Visit a museum, national park, cultural event, or historical site having to do with pre-Columbian cultures.

H. Prepare a family dinner composed entirely of foods native to the New World.

Election Day

Songs and Hymns

The Twelfth Article of Faith (*Children's Songbook* 131)
My Country (*Children's Songbook* 224)
God of Our Fathers, Whose Almighty Hand (*Hymns* 78)
Love One Another (*Hymns* 308, *Children's Songbook* 136)
America the Beautiful (*Hymns* 338)

Lesson Ideas

A. Rule by the People

Mosiah 29:26 (Do your business by the voice of the people.)
Alma 27:20-22 (The voice of the people regarding the Anti-Nephi-Lehies.)
Helaman 1:1-5 (Nephite leaders chosen by the voice of the people.)

• What arguments might be made against choosing our leaders by popular vote?

• Why is our country willing to trust the judgment of the majority in this matter?

• What responsibilities does rule by elected leaders lay on us, the citizens?

B. Electing Wise Leaders

D&C 98:8-10 (Seek for honest and wise leaders.)
D&C 134:3 (Seek for leaders who will administer equity and justice.)

• Why are so many people cynical about finding honest politicians?

• How can we tell whether a candidate will administer equity and justice?

• What resources are available for educating ourselves about candidates?

C. Overcoming Division

Matthew 5:43-45 or *3 Nephi 12:43-45* (Love your enemies.)

3 Nephi 11:29-30 (Satan stirreth up hearts to contend with anger.)
D&C 38:27 (If ye are not one ye are not mine.)
- Is it possible to have politics without contention?
- How can we love people we deeply oppose politically?
- Why is it good that there be a diversity of political views?

Discussions and Activities

A. Open the devotional with prayer, thanking God for the freedom to choose our country's leaders. Pray that we will exercise that freedom wisely and responsibly. You might also deem it appropriate to thank God for particular leaders whom you feel have discharged their offices well.

B. Make a list of the major races or issues which will be resolved in the coming election. Invite family members who are of voting age to explain how they reached a decision about who or what to vote for. To what degree do family members seek spiritual inspiration in making political decisions?

C. If a family member or friend has been active in campaigning for a candidate or issue, invite them to discuss that experience. You might ask them to address the following questions:
- Why did you decide to get so involved with this particular campaign?
- In what different capacities can people get involved in a political campaign?
- What was the most exciting thing about being involved in the campaign?
- What was the most frustrating or unpleasant aspect of the experience?
- How has your involvement affected your perception of the political process?
- Is there a connection between your political activity and your religious beliefs?

D. In the course of this devotional, it may become evident that family members have differing political views. Read D&C 38:27 and discuss the questions: Why do people tend to have strong feelings about their political differences? As a family and as a country, how can we preserve a sense of unity despite political differences?

E. Read Article of Faith 12. Point out that elections typically leave a sizable portion of voters disappointed at the results. Discuss the question: How should we respond to an administration to which we are politically opposed?

F. Read 1 Timothy 2:1-3. If you don't already, resolve to pray regularly for local, state, and national leaders in your family prayers. If you are opposed to current leaders, or if family members hold different political views, discuss what could be said in a prayer on behalf of the current administration that would be heartfelt and would reflect the feelings of all family members. Matthew 5:44-45, 3 Nephi 12:44-45 or D&C 27:18 could provide a scriptural basis for this discussion.

Veterans Day
(Armistice Day)

Songs and Hymns
Heavenly Father, Now I Pray (*Children's Songbook* 19)
Hail to the Brightness of Zion's Glad Morning (*Hymns* 42)
Behold the Mountain of the Lord (*Hymns* 54)
Father in Heaven (*Hymns* 133)
America the Beautiful (*Hymns* 338)
The Star-Spangled Banner (*Hymns* 340)

Lesson Ideas
A. Remembering Those Who Fought
Psalms 18:4-5 (The sorrows of death compassed me.)
Alma 56:15-16 (Nephite soldiers were depressed in body and spirit.)
Alma 62:41 (Many were hardened, others softened, by war.)
- What are soldiers called upon to endure?
- Why are they willing to endure all this?
- In what ways are veterans changed by war?

B. Thanks for Life
Psalms 2:1-5 (Thou, O Lord, art a shield for me.)
James 4:13-15 (If the Lord will, we shall live.)

Alma 62:48-50 (They remembered how the Lord delivered them.)
- How does Veterans Day remind us that life is a precious gift?
- What does God intend us to do with that gift?
- How can we savor more fully the life we are given?

C. An End to War

James 4:1-2 (From whence come wars and fighting?)
Alma 50:21 (The Nephites brought war upon themselves.)
Moses 6:15 (Satan raged in their hearts; from thence came wars.)
- What does it mean to say there are no winners in war?
- What do these passages of scripture suggest about how to put an end to war?
- How does Veterans Day remind us of the need to work to prevent future wars?

D. Working for Peace

Isaiah 2:3-4 or *2 Nephi 12:3-4* (Beat their swords into plowshares.)
D&C 45:68-69 (Zion will be the only people not at war.)
D&C 105:38-40 (Sue for peace to all people.)
- What would be the modern equivalents of swords and plowshares?
- Why did Isaiah speak of war as something which people "learn"?
- How can Latter-day Saints promote peace in the world?

Discussions and Activities

A. If a family member or friend is a veteran, ask him/her to speak about the experience of war. Invite him/her to focus especially on the questions: How were you changed by the experience? How has the experience changed the way you live?

B. If a family member or friend is currently serving in the armed forces, ask him/her to talk to the family about why he/she decided to serve in this way.

C. Explain to your family that Veterans Day began as Armistice Day. This day commemorated the end of World War I, which people hoped would be "the war to end all wars." Discuss the question: Why was that hope not realized? What will it take to finally put an end to war?

D. Read Matthew 5:43-44 or 3 Nephi 12:43-44. Discuss the question: After two peoples have gone to war against each other, what does it take for the survivors to come to love and forgive one another?

E. Encourage each member of the family to observe, if possible, wherever they are, a minute of silence at 11:00 on Veterans Day. Use this minute as an occasion to remember those who have suffered in war and to pray for peace.

F. As a family, make a contribution of time or money to an organization that supports veterans, or to an organization that works to promote peace.

G. In your family prayer, make special mention of any veterans, or members of the armed forces, your family knows personally. Pray on behalf of people in specific parts of the world where there is ongoing conflict.

Other Holidays

New Year

Songs and Hymns

I'm Trying to Be like Jesus (*Children's Songbook* 78)
I Want to Live the Gospel (*Children's Songbook* 148)
Be Still My Soul (*Hymns* 124)
More Holiness Give Me (*Hymns* 131)
Abide with Me! (*Hymns* 166)
Ring Out, Wild Bells (*Hymns* 215)
Come, Let Us Anew (*Hymns* 216)

Lesson Ideas

A. Reaffirming Our Covenants

2 Chronicles 34 (King Josiah and the people renewed their covenant.)

• How is a new year a chance to clean up our lives, the way Josiah purged Judah?

• How are New Year's resolutions a way of reaffirming our covenants?

• Why is it important that we periodically evaluate our lives?

B. Seeking Grace to Improve

Ezekiel 36:26-27 (A new heart will I give you.)
Ether 12:27 (I will make weak things become strong unto you.)
D&C 20:31 (Sanctification is through the grace of Jesus Christ.)

• What is the role of grace in becoming a Christlike person?

• How has grace helped members of our family grow during the past year?

• What New Year's resolutions can we make that will bring grace into our lives?

C. A Fresh Start

Colossians 3:9-14 (Ye have put off the old and put on the new.)

Mosiah 26:30 (As often as my people repent will I forgive.)

Moses 1:3-4, 38 (There is no end to my works.)

• How can we use the new year to make a fresh start on striving to be Christlike?

  • Why is God so generous about giving us fresh starts?

  • What difference does it make to know that even God is, in a sense, constantly making new beginnings (Moses 1:38)?

D. God Is Constant

Psalms 102:25-27 (All things change and wax old, but thou art the same.)

Mormon 9:9 (In God there is no variableness.)

D&C 3:1-2 (God doth not vary; his work cannot be frustrated.)

• What changes have we seen or experienced in the past year?

• How can knowing that God is constant help us face the uncertainty of change?

• As we create goals and expectations for the new year, how can we distinguish between God's will and our own?

Discussions and Activities

A. In many parts of the world, it is customary to thoroughly clean house during the days leading up to the New Year, to symbolize making a fresh start. As a family, take advantage of the Christmas vacation to tackle some major house-cleaning, in the spirit of "purging out the old" (see 1 Corinthians 5:7). At the same time, encourage family members to think about what "spiritual house-cleaning" they want to do for the New Year.

B. Invite family members to reflect in their journals on the blessings they've received during the past year and the personal growth they've experienced. Hold a personal interview with each family member to discuss your perception of his/her growth and accomplishments during the past year.

C. Invite family members to share their resolutions with each other. Discuss ways in which family members might support each other in carrying out their resolutions.

D. Read Hebrews 10:23-25. As a family, create a poster that lists (or visually represents) family traditions you resolve to begin or continue in the coming year. Place the poster someplace where it will serve as a visible reminder to all family members.

E. Along with their resolutions for the new year, have each family member make a list of regrets, disappointments, or unsuccessful plans from the old year. Read 3 Nephi 12:47. As your family rings in the new year have everyone destroy their lists of regrets, to symbolize letting go and moving on.

F. Conclude your family's celebration with prayer. Thank God for blessings received by the family during the past year. Pray that family members will be helped to remember and fulfil their New Year resolutions. Pray that they will be supported as they face the changes of the coming year.

Valentine's Day

Songs and Hymns

I Feel My Savior's Love (*Children's Songbook* 74)
Where Love Is (*Children's Songbook* 138)
I'll Walk with You (*Children's Songbook* 140)
My Heavenly Father Loves Me (*Children's Songbook* 228)
We Are Different (*Children's Songbook* 263)
God Is Love (*Hymns* 87)
Lord, I Would Follow Thee (*Hymns* 220)
Love at Home (*Hymns* 294)
O Love That Glorifies the Son (*Hymns* 295)
As I Have Loved You (*Hymns* 308, *Children's Songbook* 136)

Lesson Ideas

A. Significant Others

Genesis 2:18-24 or *Moses 3:18-24* or *Abraham 5:14-18* (They shall be one flesh.)

1 Corinthians 7:3 (Render to one another due benevolence.)

Mosiah 18:21 (Hearts knit together in love.)

• What does "benevolence" mean?

• What is involved in merging two lives into one?

• How do dating, engagement, and marriage help us progress toward that oneness?

B. Love Between Friends

Proverbs 18:24 (There is a friend that sticketh closer than a brother.)

John 15:13 (Greater love hath no man than this.)

D&C 130:2 (That same sociality which exists here will exist there.)

• Why did Jesus speak of friendship as the greatest love?

• What kind of friendship would be able to last forever?

• What difference does it make to think of Jesus Christ as a friend?

C. Let Thy Love Abound

Luke 10:25-37 (The parable of the Good Samaritan.)

Alma 1:30 (Liberal to all, having no respect to persons.)

D&C 112:11 (Be not partial; let thy love abound to all.)

• Samaritans and Jews were divided by race, religion, and the memory of past hostilities. Of whom might that be said for us today?

• Why do we have a hard time loving some people?

• How can we show—not just talk about—love for all people?

D. Christlike Love

John 13:34 (As I have loved you, love one another.)

Moroni 7:47-48 (Pray that ye may be filled with this love.)

D&C 88:123 (Learn to impart one to another.)

• How did—or does—Christ show his love for others?

• Is Christlike love something we feel, or is it something we do?

• Why do we have to pray for Christlike love?

E. The God of Love

1 John 4:8-11 (God is love.)

2 Nephi 1:15 (Encircled about eternally in the arms of his love.)

2 Nephi 26:24-25 (He loveth the world.)

D&C 18:10 (The worth of souls.)

• When have family members felt God's love for them?

• How does knowing that God loves us unconditionally inspire us to be all we can?

• How can we practice unconditional love in our relationships with others?

Discussions and Activities

A. Use Valentines Day as a chance to reflect (perhaps in your journal) on your relationships with family, friends, and others. Take steps to strengthen those relationships: giving up grudges, strengthening ties, spending more time with loved ones, and so on.

B. Make—not buy—a valentine for every member of your family. In these valentines, list or visually represent ways in which family members have shown their love for you during the past year.

C. Invite each family member to make a valentine for God or for the Savior. This can be a way for family members to reflect on their love for our Heavenly Father or for Jesus. Arrange these valentines someplace where family members can see them frequently, perhaps in the place where family prayer is held.

D. In some parts of the world, Valentines Day is celebrated as Friendship Day. Invite family members to find ways to express appreciation for their close friends.

E. List as many answers as you can think of to the question: What do we mean when we say, "I love you"? Couch your answers as statements beginning with "I." For instance:

- I enjoy spending time with you.
- I want to help you achieve your goals.
- I get indignant when I see people hurting you.
- I'm happy to provide a listening ear.
- I think of your problems as my problems.
- I'm willing to be patient when you drive me crazy.

F. Discuss the questions: What would a relationship (family, marriage, friendship) based on conditional love look like? What would one based on unconditional love look like?

G. If family members are approaching dating age, use Valentines Day as an opportunity to teach them about romance. Song of Solomon 2:10-13; 5:2-5; and 7:11-13 could serve as the opening for this discussion. Questions to consider might include:

- What is the role of romance in strengthening love?
- At what point in a dating relationship does romance become appropriate?
- How does one cultivate romance?

• Besides romance, what else goes into making a strong relationship?

• Does our society place undue emphasis on romance?

H. Obtain a copy of the Statement of the First Presidency regarding God's Love for All Mankind, issued February 15, 1978. (The statement was reprinted in the *Ensign*, Jan. 1988, p. 48). As a family, copy out notable phrases and sentences from the statement onto heart-shaped cutouts, as if they were valentines from Heavenly Father to his children.

I. Point out that D&C 76 (the vision of the three degrees of glory) was revealed two days after Valentines Day. Read the vision in its entirety and discuss the question: What do we learn from this vision about God's love?

J. Celebrate Valentines Day by carrying out a special service project for someone in need, or by reaching out to someone who is lonely.

K. Read D&C 112:11. As a family, resolve that during the coming year you will take an active concern in the needs of a particular group of people outside your usual circle. This might be the people of a country where a family member is serving a mission, or a particular group in need within your own community. Make plans to learn more about the group's needs and how your family might help.

L. Use the closing prayer as an opportunity to express your family's love for God and for one another. Pray to be filled with Christlike love (see Moroni 7:48).

Halloween

Note: Like Christmas and Easter, Halloween began as a religious holiday but has since been heavily secularized. The following devotional ideas are meant to highlight the holiday's religious significance, which is connected with remembering the dead.

Songs and Hymns
Truth from Elijah (*Children's Songbook* 90)
The Hearts of the Children (*Children's Songbook* 92)
Family History—I Am Doing It (*Children's Songbook* 94)

It's Autumntime (*Children's Songbook* 246)
Autumn Day (*Children's Songbook* 247)
How Beautiful Thy Temples, Lord (*Hymns* 288)
Turn Your Hearts (*Hymns* 291)
Each Life That Touches Ours for Good (*Hymns* 293)

Lesson Ideas

A. A Merry Heart

Proverbs 17:22 (A merry heart doeth good like a medicine.)
Colossians 2:16 (Let no one judge you in respect of any holiday.)
D&C 59:18 (All things of the earth are made to gladden the heart.)

- Why do some people hesitate or refuse to celebrate Halloween?
- What does our family enjoy about Halloween?
- How does our Halloween celebration use things of the earth to "gladden the heart"?

B. Traditions from Long Ago

Deuteronomy 32:7 (Remember the days of old.)
Luke 2:42 (Jesus' parents taught him holiday customs.)
Malachi 4:5-6 or *3 Nephi 25:5-6* (The hearts of the children.)

- How did traditions such as carving pumpkins, wearing costumes, and begging for sweets get started?
- Do these traditions mean the same thing to us today that they did to people long ago?
- What is the value of preserving traditions such as these?

C. Remembering the Dead

Malachi 4:5-6 or *3 Nephi 25:5-6* (The hearts of the children.)
Luke 20:38 (He is not a God of the dead; all live unto him.)
D&C 130:2 (That same sociality which exists here will exist there.)

- Many Halloween traditions grow out of ancient customs for remembering the dead. Why is it important for people to have such customs?
- How and why do Latter-day Saints remember the dead?
- What difference does it make to know that the dead, and our relationships with them, go on?

D. Redeeming the Dead

1 Corinthians 15:29 (What shall they do which are baptized for the dead?)

D&C 128:15 (They without us cannot be made perfect.)

D&C 138:32-37 (Thus was the gospel preached to the dead.)

• For many Christians around the world, Halloween is a time for praying on behalf of the dead. What do Latter-day Saints do on behalf of the dead?

• What blessings do family history and temple work bring to the living?

• How does work for the dead attest to God's love for all?

Discussions and Activities

A. On or near October 3, read D&C 138 with your family. Invite family members to dedicate the month of October to remembering the dead through family history and temple work. Special projects for this month might include organizing scrapbooks, preparing names for ordinance work, or spending more time at the temple.

B. Explain that throughout history, people have felt a need to remember the dead. Many Halloween traditions originally arose for that purpose, although today we celebrate them just for fun. Discuss the question: How does the restored gospel help us understand why people all over the world would feel a need to remember the dead?

C. Explain to your family (1) that many of our Halloween traditions originated among non-Christian peoples, and (2) that because of this fact, some Christians do not celebrate Halloween, regarding it as inspired by the devil. Discuss the question: Do the teachings of the restored gospel require Latter-day Saints to take such a hostile stance toward non-Christian cultures and customs?

D. Explain that harvest festivals were an important part of religious life for the Lord's people long ago (see, for instance, Exodus 34:22). Discuss the question: How can our family use Halloween as an opportunity to celebrate the harvest and the coming of autumn?

E. The word "Halloween" comes from All Hallows Eve, which is the night before All Saints Day (November 1) and All Souls Day (November 2). For many Christians around the world, this is a time to hold services in memory of the dead and to visit loved ones' graves. Consider taking this opportunity to visit or remember your own departed loved ones (see "Ideas for a Memorial," in the section of this book titled "Death of a Family Member").

Thanksgiving

Songs and Hymns

Can a Little Child like Me? (*Children's Songbook* 9)
A Song of Thanks (*Children's Songbook* 20)
Thanks to Our Father (*Children's Songbook* 20)
For Health and Strength (*Children's Songbook* 21)
For Thy Bounteous Blessings (*Children's Songbook* 21)
For the Beauty of the Earth (*Hymns* 92)
Prayer of Thanksgiving (*Hymns* 93)
Come, Ye Thankful People (*Hymns* 94)
Now Thank We All Our God (*Hymns* 95)

Lesson Ideas

A. Praise and Thanksgiving

Psalms 69:30 (I will magnify God with thanksgiving.)
Alma 26:8 (Let us sing to his praise and give thanks.)
D&C 136:28 (Praise the Lord with singing, music, thanksgiving.)
• In what sense is thanksgiving an act of praise?
• What would a "prayer of praise" (D&C 136:28) sound like?
• Why do the scriptures so often connect praise and thanksgiving to song?

B. In Every Thing Give Thanks

1 Thessalonians 5:18 (In every thing give thanks.)
Alma 7:23 (Return thanks for whatsoever ye receive.)
D&C 98:1-3 (Your afflictions shall work together for your good.)
• What difficulties has our family faced during the past year?
• Can we find it in ourselves to give thanks for those difficulties?
• How have we been blessed in spite of our difficulties?

C. The Gifts of Providence

Joel 2:26 (Praise God, that hath dealt wondrously with you.)
Jacob 3:13 (Providence hath smiled upon you most pleasantly.)

Mosiah 2:20-21 (God preserves you from day to day.)
- In what ways has God "dealt wondrously" with our family?
- To what degree does our prosperity result from factors we have no control over?
- What difference does it make to know that everything we have is a gift?

D. Sharing Our Bounty
Luke 3:10-11 (He that hath two coats, let him impart.)
Mosiah 4:16 (Administer of your substance to those in need.)
D&C 104:14-18 (Impart of the abundance which I have made.)
- Why is there so much poverty and hunger in the world?
- In what ways does our family share our abundance with others?
- What could we do in this coming year to share even more generously?

Discussions and Activities

A. Ask each family member to come to Thanksgiving dinner with a passage of scripture which expresses praise or thanksgiving. Read these passages before praying over the food.

B. Give each family member five kernels of corn. Explain that during the Pilgrims' first winter in the New World, conditions became so bad that each person had to make do with a daily ration of five kernels of corn. (See Sterling W. Sill, *The Glory of the Sun*, p. 90.)

Go around the table, having each family member hold up one of their kernels while they state one thing they are thankful for. Go around the table five times so that each person in your family expresses thanks for five different things.

C. At some point in your Thanksgiving observance, spend some time singing hymns of praise and thanksgiving together.

D. As a family, compose your own psalm of praise and thanksgiving. You may find these simple models useful.

- Model 1. (Psalm 148.) Begin with the line, "Praise ye the Lord." Then compose a series of lines, each beginning with the words, "Praise ye him," followed by the name of some specific creation, or pair of creations. For example:

Praise ye him, ducks and geese.
Praise ye him, maple and oak trees.
Praise ye him, geysers and hot springs.
Praise ye him, currents of electricity.
End as you began, with the line, "Praise ye the Lord."

• Model 2. (Psalm 147.) Start with the line, "Praise the Lord, for he works righteousness forever." Then add lines describing different ways in which the Lord's power, grandeur, and goodness are revealed. For example:

He makes black holes and supernovas.
He knows personally every ant on earth.
He gives artists the talent to make beautiful things.
He loves us even when we forget him.
End with the line, "Praise ye the Lord."

• Model 3. (Psalm 136.) Start with the line, "Give thanks unto the Lord; for his mercy endures forever." Then list things that the Lord has done to help your family, your ancestors, or people in general. End each line with the phrase "for his mercy endures forever." For example:

He helped Grandma recover from her surgery:
for his mercy endures forever.
He brought our ancestors safely to this country:
for his mercy endures forever.
He gave us the scriptures to guide us:
for his mercy endures forever.
He gave us vaccines to protect us from disease:
for his mercy endures forever.
End by repeating the line, "Give thanks unto the Lord; for his mercy endures forever."

E. Read Ephesians 1:16. Discuss the question: How is it possible to always be giving thanks to God?

F. Read the Pharisee's prayer from Luke 18:11 and the Zoramites' prayer from Alma 31:16-18. Discuss the question: What is wrong with the thanksgiving offered by the Pharisee and the Zoramites?

G. Write a note for each member of your family, thanking him/her for ways in which he/she has helped you or blessed your life in the past year.

H. Invite someone you know will spend Thanksgiving alone to participate in your family's celebration.

I. As a family, make a thanksgiving offering of money, time, food-stuffs, or clothing to a program that serves the needy.

Ethnic or Cultural Celebrations

Songs and Hymns
I'm Thankful to Be Me (*Children's Songbook* 11)
Children All Over the World (*Children's Songbook* 16)
Truth from Elijah (*Children's Songbook* 90)
The Hearts of the Children (*Children's Songbook* 92)
We Are Different (*Children's Songbook* 263)
O God, Our Help in Ages Past (*Hymns* 31)
Behold, the Mountain of the Lord (*Hymns* 54)

Lesson Ideas
A. Remembering Our Heritage
Deuteronomy 32:7 (Remember the days of old.)
Ether 6:30 (Orihah remembered what God did for his ancestors.)
Malachi 4:5-6 or *3 Nephi 25:5-6* (The hearts of the children.)
• What is the value of remembering our ethnic or cultural her-itage?
• How has God blessed our ancestral people?
• How do ethnic or cultural celebrations help turn the children's hearts to the fathers?

B. God Hath Made All Nations
Acts 17:24-26 (God hath made all nations.)
Revelation 4:11 (Thou hast created all things for thy pleasure.)
Genesis 1:31 or *Moses 2:31* (Everything God made was good.)
• Why would God find pleasure in creating a diversity of peoples and cultures?

• How is our world both blessed and challenged by this diversity?

• How is an ethnic or cultural celebration a way of rejoicing in God's creation?

C. The Blessing of Identity

Revelation 7:9-10 (A multitude of all nations stood before the throne.)

Alma 11:42-44 (Our bodies will rise even as they are now.)

D&C 130:2 (The same sociality which exists here will exist there.)

• What do these passages suggest about ethnic and cultural identity in relation to the resurrection?

• How does our ethnic or cultural background contribute to who we are?

• How is our family's ethnic or cultural identity a blessing to us?

Discussions and Activities

A. As a family, create a definition of "culture." Discuss the questions: What role does culture play in our mortal and eternal development? How do cultural celebrations help preserve a culture from one generation to the next?

B. As a family, create a poster depicting ethnic or cultural traditions that enrich your family's life, or that you have recently discovered and would like to revive within your family. Label the poster, "Hold the traditions which ye have been taught" (2 Thessalonians 2:15).

C. Read Alma 29:8 and D&C 10:52. Discuss the question: How does the restored gospel reinforce or build on the values of our ethnic or cultural heritage?

D. Read Isaiah 2:2 (2 Nephi 12:2). Review the history of how the restored gospel has spread among people of your ethnicity or nationality. Discuss the questions: How does the restored gospel speak to the particular values, concerns, and aspirations of people from our ethnic or national background? How is the restored church enriched by members of our ethnic or cultural background?

E. Ask family members to think of examples from current events in which people have directed prejudice or violence against members of another ethnic or cultural group. Then read Acts 10:34. Discuss the question: How can ethnic or cultural celebrations serve as occasions to promote understanding and respect for all people?

F. In the spirit of D&C 93:53, attend a celebration connected with an ethnicity or culture other than your own. Before attending the event, research the customs and history of the other culture.

G. During the closing prayer, thank God for the blessing of your family's ethnic or cultural heritage. Include thanks for your ancestors—the struggles they made on behalf of their descendants and the values which they passed down through generations. Pray that family members will preserve and honor this heritage.

Times of Our Lives

Naming and Blessing of Children

Songs and Hymns

I Thank Thee, Dear Father (*Children's Songbook* 7)

I Think When I Read That Sweet Story (*Children's Songbook* 56)

Jesus Loved the Little Children (*Children's Songbook* 59)

I Am a Child of God (*Hymns* 301, *Children's Songbook* 2)

I Know My Father Lives (*Hymns* 302, *Children's Songbook* 5)

Teach Me to Walk in the Light (*Hymns* 304, *Children's Songbook* 177)

As I Have Loved You (*Hymns* 308, *Children's Songbook* 136)

Lesson Ideas

A. Jesus Blessed the Children

Mark 10:13-16 (Suffer little children to come unto me.)

3 Nephi 17:11-25 (Jesus blessed the children in the New World.)

D&C 20:70 (Church members should bring their children to be blessed.)

• What do we learn from these stories about Jesus' love for children?

• What do you imagine Jesus might have said when he blessed the children?

• Why does the Savior want children to be blessed?

B. Bringing up Children in Light

Mosiah 4:14-15 (Teach your children to love one another.)

D&C 68:25-28 (Teach your children to pray and to walk uprightly.)

D&C 93:38-40 (Bring up your children in light and truth.)

• What do we learn from these scriptures about our responsibilities as parents?

• What family traditions can help our children grow close to God?

• How does a baby blessing help bring light into a child's life?

C. Welcoming a New Member of the Family

Psalms 127:3 (Children are a gift from the Lord.)

Mark 9:36-37 (Whosoever receiveth a child receiveth me.)

1 Thessalonians 3:12 (The Lord make you to increase in love.)

• In what ways is this new baby a gift to our family?

• How can we extend our love to this new member of our family?

• How does a baby blessing serve as an expression of our family's love?

D. A Child of God Begins Earth Life

Deuteronomy 6:4-7 (Love the Lord thy God; teach these words to thy children.)

Acts 17:24-28 (We are God's offspring.)

D&C 101:38 (Seek the Lord always, and ye shall have eternal life.)

• What does it mean to say that we "feel after" God (Acts 17:27)?

• What can our family do to help this child develop love for our Heavenly Father and a desire to know him?

• Why does Father in Heaven want his children to be blessed as they begin earth life?

E. A Name and a Blessing

John 10:2-3, 14 (The Good Shepherd calls his sheep by name.)

Helaman 5:6 (Why Nephi and Lehi received their names.)

• Why was each member of the family given the name he/she received?

• What name will the new baby be blessed with, and why was this name chosen?

• What difference does it make to realize that the Savior knows each of us by name?

Discussions and Activities

A. During the opening prayer, offer thanks for the gift of this new child. Thank God for watching over both mother and child throughout the pregnancy and during the delivery.

B. Read 3 Nephi 17:21, noting that when Jesus blessed the children, he also prayed for them. Ask family members what hopes or wishes they would extend to this new member of the family. Allow family members time to reflect silently on the question and to voice their thoughts, if they wish. (Alternatively, each family member could write their answers, perhaps in the form of a letter to the baby.)

C. Give each member of the family a chance to hold or touch the baby and to welcome the baby aloud into the family. To their welcome, each family member could add a personal promise to help care for and raise this child.

D. Recall the blessings given to other family members when they were infants. Discuss ways in which you see those blessing being fulfilled. Encourage family members to be attentive to the blessings that will soon be given to the new baby. After the blessing, each family member could create a drawing to represent one of the blessings given to the new baby. These drawings could be preserved in a scrapbook.

E. This might be an appropriate time to discuss the changes that have come to the household as a result of the new baby's arrival. What new responsibilities have family members acquired? What concerns have arisen? Young children especially need to be reassured that while the new baby may demand more of the parents' time, other family members are no less loved.

F. Family members might consider fasting with the person who will give the baby blessing, as he seeks for inspiration.

Baptism and Confirmation

Songs and Hymns

Baptism (*Children's Songbook* 100)
When Jesus Christ Was Baptized (*Children's Songbook* 102)
The Holy Ghost (*Children's Songbook* 105)

Listen, Listen (*Children's Songbook* 107)
Come, Follow Me (*Hymns* 116)
Let the Holy Spirit Guide (*Hymns* 143)
Father in Heaven, We Do Believe (*Hymns* 180)

Lesson Ideas
A. Following Jesus into the Water
Matthew 3:13-17 (Jesus was baptized.)
2 Nephi 31:11-13 (Follow your Savior down into the water.)
3 Nephi 27:20-21 (Do the works which you have seen me do.)
• What difference does it make to realize that when we are baptized, we are doing something that Jesus himself did?
• In what ways do members of our family do the works that Jesus did?
• How does the gift of the Holy Ghost help us follow Jesus' example?

B. The Baptismal Covenant
Mosiah 18:7-16 (Alma explains the baptismal covenant.)
• What promises do we make to God when we are baptized?
• What promises does God make to us?
• How do our family's traditions help us live out the baptismal covenant?

C. Beginning a New Life
Romans 6:3-4 (By baptism we are raised to newness of life.)
2 Corinthians 5:17 (Those who are in Christ are new creatures.)
Moses 6:58-62 (We are born again of blood, water, and the Spirit.)
• How do baptism and confirmation symbolize a second birth?
• In what ways does baptism entail adopting a new way of life?
• How does the gift of the Holy Ghost help us live in a different way?

D. Walking in the Spirit
3 Nephi 27:20 (Be baptized so that you may receive the Holy Ghost.)
D&C 11:12-13 (Put your trust in that Spirit which leadeth to do good.)

Galatians 5:22-23, 25 (The fruits of the Spirit; let us walk in the Spirit.)

Jeremiah 31:31-34 (I will write my law in their hearts; they shall know me.)

• What do we learn from these scriptures about the influence of the Holy Ghost?

• How do we cultivate the fruits of the Spirit in our home?

• How do baptism and confirmation help us deepen our relationship with God?

E. Becoming Children of Christ

Mosiah 5:7-9 (Because of the covenant, ye are children of Christ.)
Moroni 6:3 (Those who are baptized take on the name of Christ.)
D&C 50:40-41 (Fear not little children; ye must grow in grace.)

• What does it mean to be a child of Christ?

• What does it mean to grow in grace?

• How do baptism and confirmation help us live with greater confidence?

F. Numbered among God's People

Mosiah 25:23-24 (Those who take Christ's name become God's people.)

Moroni 6:3-6 (The people of Christ's church nourished one another.)

Moses 7:18 (Why the Lord called his people ZION.)

• What do we learn from this passages about what it means to be God's people?

• How does our family strive to live worthy to be counted among God's people?

• How does baptism entail a commitment to serve God and others?

Discussions and Activities

A. Write the terms of the baptismal covenant (Mosiah 18:8-10) on a large piece of paper, as if it were a contract signed by Jesus. After discussing the covenant, ask the family member who is to be baptized to come forward to sign the contract. (The same piece of paper might be stored and brought out every time a family member is baptized, until the entire family has signed their names.)

B. Invite each family member who has been baptized to express his/her testimony in the form of a letter to the person being baptized. Encourage family members to focus in their letters on the role that the baptismal covenant and the gift of the Holy Ghost play in their lives.

C. As a family, create a poster with the slogan, "I want to follow Jesus' example." Add drawings, family photographs, pictures from Church magazines, and so on, that illustrate this theme. At the close of the devotional, hang the poster in the room of the person being baptized. (Alternative ideas for slogans include: "I want to keep my baptismal covenants," "I want to walk in the Spirit," "I want to grow in grace," or "I want to serve God and my neighbor.")

D. Ask family members to reflect (either silently or aloud) on things that make them feel afraid, overwhelmed, or inadequate. Read D&C 50:40-44. Discuss the questions: How do baptism and confirmation give us the spiritual power to face troubles with confidence? How do these ordinances provide assurance of God's love for each of us?

E. Recall the blessings and admonitions given to other family members when they were confirmed. Encourage family members to pay attention to what is said during the upcoming confirmation. After the confirmation, each family member could create a drawing to represent one of the blessings or admonitions given to the newly baptized person. These drawings could be preserved with the person's scrapbook or journal.

F. Give each family member the opportunity to express their hopes or wishes on behalf of the person who is to be baptized.

G. If the devotional is being held in advance of the baptismal service, this might be an appropriate time to discuss what part family members will play in the service.

H. Family members might consider fasting with the person who will perform the confirmation, as he seeks inspiration.

I. If the climate and weather permit, consider arranging to perform the baptism in some secluded spot outdoors.

J. While the ordinances of baptism and confirmation are naturally solemn occasions, this is also a time for rejoicing and therefore celebration. On the night before the baptism, or after returning home from the baptismal service, celebrate the occasion with a special activity, meal, or dessert.

K. Encourage family members who have already been baptized to use this occasion to reflect in their journals about their discipleship. Family members who have not yet been baptized could be helped to reflect on how they are preparing for baptism.

Becoming a Beehive

Songs and Hymns

Search, Ponder, and Pray (*Children's Songbook* 109)
I Will Be Valiant (*Children's Songbook* 162)
I Will Follow God's Plan (*Children's Songbook* 164)
As Zion's Youth in Latter Days (*Hymns* 256)
As I Search the Holy Scriptures (*Hymns* 277)
I Am a Child of God (*Hymns* 301, *Children's Songbook* 2)
I Know My Father Lives (*Hymns* 302, *Children's Songbook* 5)

Lesson Ideas

A. A Young Woman of Truth

2 Nephi 32:5 (The Holy Ghost will show you what to do.)
Alma 5:46 (I have prayed many days to know these things of myself.)
Ether 4:11 (The Spirit persuadeth to do good.)
Moroni 10:5 (By the Holy Ghost you may know the truth of all things.)

• What do we learn from these passages about the Spirit's influence in our lives?

• As our family member moves into adolescence, why is it important for her to develop her own testimony?

• How will her experiences as a Beehive foster her personal spirituality?

B. Stand for Truth and Righteousness

Matthew 5:16 or *3 Nephi 12:16* (Let your light so shine.)
1 Timothy 4:12 (Be thou an example.)
D&C 115:5 (Be a standard for the nations.)

• When have we seen our family member serve as an example of Christlike behavior?

• As a Beehive, what opportunities will she have to share God's light with others?

• How can a 12-year-old stand for truth and righteousness?

C. Divine Nature

2 Peter 1:2-8 (Partakers of the divine nature.)

Alma 7:23-24 (Alma's exhortation to the Gideonites.)

D&C 121:45-46 (Let thy bowels be full of charity towards all.)

• How do the physical, mental, and social development we experience during adolescence make us more like our heavenly parents?

• What divine qualities are listed in these passages of scripture?

• As a Beehive, how can our family member further develop these qualities?

D. Choice and Accountability

1 Nephi 15:8 (Have ye inquired of the Lord?)

2 Nephi 32:3 (Feast upon the words of Christ.)

Alma 37:37 (Counsel with the Lord in all thy doings.)

3 Nephi 18:20 (Whatever you ask, which is right, you shall receive.)

D&C 9:7-9 (How to seek and recognize inspiration.)

• Why is learning to make wise choices an important part of adolescence?

• What do these passages teach us about making choices and solving problems?

• How will our family member's experiences as a Beehive teach her accountability?

E. Embarking in God's Service

Matthew 5:16 (That they may see your good works.)

Matthew 25:34-40 (The parable of the sheep and the goats.)

Mosiah 2:17 (To serve your fellow beings is to serve God.)

D&C 4:1-3 (O ye that embark in the service of God.)

• In what sense is our new Beehive embarking in God's service?

• What do we learn from these passages about how to serve God?

• As a Beehive, what opportunities will our family member have to serve others?

Discussions and Activities

A. Consider inviting your family member's new Young Women leader to participate in the devotional. Give the leader the opportunity to express her support for your family member and to welcome your family member into Beehives.

B. In advance, help the new Beehive memorize the Young Women Theme. During the devotional, have her recite the theme, together with all other family members who are or have been in Young Women.

C. Display the Young Women Logo and Motto. Ask family members to reflect (perhaps in their journals) on the ways in which they each stand for truth and righteousness in their own lives.

D. Prepare a brief presentation on the Young Women values and their colors. (It would be especially appropriate for this presentation to be made by other family members who have been in Young Women.) Invite family members—male and female—to testify about the role these values play in their lives.

Then show your family the Young Women Personal Progress booklet. Explain that as a Beehive, and throughout her time in Young Women, your family member will complete Value Experiences related to each of the Young Women values. As a family, you might create a poster-sized version of the "Personal Progress Record Sheet" to display someplace where family members can see it often.

E. Prepare a brief presentation on the Beehive mission statement and symbol. Invite family members—male and female—to testify about the direction they receive from the Holy Ghost.

F. In advance, ask your family member to complete the following sentences. If she wants, she might prepare a collage to represent her answers visually.

- When I picture in my mind who God is, I see . . .
- I believe following Christ means . . .
- What I value about being a member of the Church is . . .
- I believe I'm on earth in order to . . .
- I believe the absolute most important things in life are . . .
- I feel good about myself as a person when . . .

During the devotional, have your family member read her completed sentences, or interpret her collage, to the rest of the family.

Point out that what she has just shared is her testimony. Discuss how your family member's experiences in Young Women will help her further develop her testimony of the restored gospel.

G. Review the various Value Experiences listed in the Young Women Personal Progress booklet. Take note of Value Experiences which could be carried out in a family devotional or home evening. Read Mosiah 4:27. Resolve that on a regular, periodic basis, you and your family member will plan a devotional or home evening related to one of the Value Experiences.

H. Give each family member the opportunity to voice their congratulations, hopes, or wishes to the new Beehive.

I. In lieu of a prayer, consider closing with a priesthood blessing for the new Beehive.

Ideas for Individual Instruction

This would be an especially appropriate occasion for an individual discussion with your family member about the challenges and opportunities of adolescence.

A. Read 2 Peter 2:2-4 and paragraph 2 of the Proclamation on the Family ("All human beings—male and female—are created in the image of God. Each is a beloved spirit son or daughter of heavenly parents, and, as such, each has a divine nature and destiny"). Explain that the physical changes which accompany adolescence—including sexual development—make us more like our heavenly parents.

Find out how your family member feels about her physical development. Take the time to answer questions she may have. Let her know how excited you are to see her beginning the transition from childhood to adulthood.

B. Read JS-H 1:28. Discuss the importance of making friends who respect our values and support us in the pursuit of our goals, especially during the adolescent years. Then read Proverbs 17:17 and 2 Nephi 1:30. Together, brainstorm a list of the qualities of a true friend. Help your family member think of ways in which she could demonstrate these qualities in her friendships.

As part of your discussion of friendship, review what the law of chastity teaches us about appropriate relationships. It may be helpful to read together from the pamphlet, *For the Strength of Youth*. Revisit the rules that govern your family member's interaction with friends (for instance, curfews). Make whatever adjustments to the rules seem appropriate to your family member's developing maturity.

C. Read Proverbs 4:13 and D&C 93:36. Find out what aspirations your family member has for her adult life. Discuss the importance of education in helping her pursue her dreams and develop her potential, especially during her adolescent years. Praise your family member for her progress in school. Discuss concerns you or she may have (grades that need improving, the transition into middle school or junior high, and so on).

D. Discuss the exciting opportunities that await your family member during her adolescent years. Then discuss the kinds of hurt, frustration, stress, and insecurity adolescence might bring. Read Psalms 71:1-7 and Alma 37:35-37. Help your family member set up a program of regular personal scripture study and prayer. Testify of the role that prayer and the scriptures play in helping you face challenges and adversity.

Becoming a Mia Maid

Songs and Hymns
I'm Trying to Be like Jesus (*Children's Songbook* 78)
I Will Be Valiant (*Children's Songbook* 162)
I Will Follow God's Plan (*Children's Songbook* 164)
More Holiness Give Me (*Hymns* 131)
Lord, I Would Follow *Thee* (*Hymns* 220)
As Zion's Youth in Latter Days (*Hymns* 256)
O My Father (*Hymns* 292)

Lesson Ideas
A. A Young Woman of Promise
Mosiah 5:7 (Because of the covenant, ye are children of Christ.)
Mosiah 18:8-10, 21 (The conditions of the baptismal covenant.)
Matthew 5:9 (The peacemakers shall be called children of God.)
Matthew 22:37-39 (The first and second great commandments.)
John 15:12-13 (This is my commandment, that ye love one another.)

• When have we seen our family member living out her baptismal covenant?

• How will caring relationships with others help our family member face the challenges of adolescence?

• How will her experiences as a Mia Maid further foster her spirituality?

B. Stand for Truth and Righteousness

Matthew 5:16 or *3 Nephi 12:16* (Let your light so shine.)

Mosiah 18:9 (Stand as witnesses of God at all times.)

D&C 124:15, 20 (The Lord commended the integrity of early Saints.)

• What situations might a 14-year-old face which require integrity?

• When have we seen our family member stand for truth and righteousness?

• How is building caring relationships a way of standing as a witness of God?

C. Divine Nature

2 Peter 1:2-8 (Partakers of the divine nature.)

1 John 4:7-8 (Every one that loveth knoweth God, for God is love.)

Moroni 7:48 (If we are filled with love, we will be like Christ.)

• When have we seen our family member exhibit the qualities listed in 2 Peter 1:5-7?

• How will living the Mia Maid mission statement help her become more Christlike?

• Why is it necessary to pray for love?

D. Choice and Accountability

2 Nephi 2:11, 15-16, 27-28 (We are free to act for ourselves.)

• As our new Mia Maid matures, what new freedoms and privileges will she enjoy?

• What examples do we see in today's world of teenagers making unwise choices?

• When have we seen our family member exercise responsibility?

E. Persevering in Service

D&C 6:8-10 (You shall be the means of doing much good.)
D&C 46:11-12 (Every one has a spiritual gift.)
D&C 58:27-28 (Be anxiously engaged in a good cause.)
- What talents or gifts has our family member been blessed with?
- When have we seen her using her gifts to serve others?
- As a Mia Maid, what opportunities will she have to do good in the world?

Discussions and Activities

A. Consider inviting your family member's new Young Women leader to participate in the devotional. Give the leader the opportunity to express her support for your family member and to welcome your family member into Mia Maids.

B. Display the Young Women Logo and Motto. Near the start of the devotional, ask family members who are, or have been, in Young Women to recite the Young Women theme together.

C. Create a poster listing the Young Women values with their respective colors. Ask family members to name ways in which they've seen the new Mia Maid demonstrate or cultivate these values. Read D&C 93:13 and discuss the question: Why is cultivating these values a lifelong goal for all of us?

D. Prepare a brief presentation on the Mia Maid mission statement and symbol. Invite family members—male and female—to testify about the role of any of the following in their lives:
- The baptismal covenant.
- Caring relationships with others.
- The Spirit.
- The scriptures.

E. Ask your family member to recount a few of the Value Experiences or Projects she completed as a Beehive, focusing especially on experiences in which other family members participated. Then ask your family member to identify some of the Value Experiences or Projects she wants to complete during her time as a Mia Maid. Discuss ways in which other family members can support her as she continues to work on Personal Progress.

F. From the Young Women Personal Progress booklet, review the list of Value Experiences your family member still needs to complete. Take note of Value Experiences which could be carried out in a family devotional or home evening. Read Mosiah 4:27. Resolve that on a regular, periodic basis, you and your family member will plan a devotional or home evening related to one of the Value Experiences.

G. Give each family member the opportunity to voice their congratulations, hopes, or wishes to the new Mia Maid.

H. In lieu of a prayer, consider closing with a priesthood blessing for the new Mia Maid.

Ideas for Individual Instruction

This would be an especially appropriate occasion for an individual discussion with your family member about the on-going challenges and opportunities of adolescence.

A. Read Psalms 139:14 and Moses 2:27, 31. Point out that many teenagers feel embarrassment or anxiety because of the physical effects of puberty (acne, awkward growth spurts, and so on). Discuss the question: What do these scriptures tell your family member about her body?

Together, make a list of behaviors that abuse the body (drug use, unhealthy eating habits, and so on). Discuss the questions: What pressures lead some teenagers to engage in these behaviors? What better ways are there to react to those pressures?

B. Read John 15:12-13. Describe for your family member your notion of an ideal friend, and invite her to do the same. Commend your family member for specific moments in which you've seen her be a supportive friend. Testify about the role that good friends played in helping you face the challenges of adolescence.

As part of your discussion of friendship, review what the law of chastity teaches us about appropriate relationships. It may be helpful to read together from the pamphlet, *For the Strength of Youth*. Revisit the rules that govern your family member's interaction with friends (for instance, curfews). Make whatever adjustments to the rules seem appropriate to your family member's developing maturity.

C. Read D&C 88:118. Commend your family member for specific ways in which you've seen her increase in knowledge, both spiritual and secular, during the last two years. Since your family member will probably enroll in seminary at some point during her

Mia Maid years, discuss the role of seminary in her on-going search to learn "by faith."

D. Read Psalms 71:1-7 and Alma 37:35-37. Invite your family member to discuss some of the challenges she's faced during the past two years. What has helped her confront those challenges? Commend your family member for ways in which you've seen her develop spiritual strength.

Follow up on your family member's program of personal scripture study and invite her to set new scripture study goals for the coming year. Testify of how a close relationship with Heavenly Father helps you face challenges and adversity.

Becoming a Laurel

Songs and Hymns

I Love to See the Temple (*Children's Songbook* 95)
Faith (*Children's Songbook* 96)
I Will Be Valiant (*Children's Songbook* 162)
I Will Follow God's Plan (*Children's Songbook* 164)
Our Savior's Love (*Hymns* 113)
When Faith Endures (*Hymns* 128)
As Zion's Youth in Latter Days (*Hymns* 256)

Lesson Ideas

A. A Young Woman of Faith

D&C 136:4 (We will walk in all the ordinances of the Lord.)

Articles of Faith 1:3 (All may be saved through gospel ordinances.)

Alma 7:14 (See that ye have faith, hope, and charity.)

• How does faith give our family member confidence and direction in life?

• How have we seen gospel ordinances bring spiritual power into her life?

• What will she do as a Laurel to prepare herself for the ordinances of the temple?

B. Stand for Truth and Righteousness

John 13:34 (By this shall all know ye are my disciples.)
Mosiah 18:8-9 (Stand as witnesses of God at all times.)
Alma 5:33-34 (The Lord's arms are extended towards all.)
• How is showing love a way of standing as a witness of God?
• When have we seen our family member act out of love for others?
• What opportunities does a Laurel have to reach out to others, as the Savior did?

C. Divine Nature

Alma 5:11-16, 26-28 (Have ye experienced this mighty change?)
• How have we seen our family member become more Christlike over the last four years?
• When have we seen her bring forth "works of righteousness"?
• How will preparing for temple ordinances help her fulfill her divine mission?

D. Choice and Accountability

2 Nephi 32:5 (The Holy Ghost will show you what ye should do.)
Alma 37:37 (Counsel with the Lord in all thy doings.)
D&C 6:14-15 (Thou hast been enlightened by the Spirit.)
• What major life decisions will our family member make during her Laurel years?
• How have her experiences in Young Women helped prepare her to make these decisions wisely?
• What other resources are available to help her make these decisions?

E. Living and Sharing the Gospel

D&C 6:8-9 (You shall be the means of doing much good.)
D&C 18:15 (If you bring save it be but one soul to me.)
D&C 88:77 (Teach one another the doctrine of the kingdom.)
• How can a 16-year-old make a difference in the world?
• What opportunities does a Laurel have to help bring others closer to God?
• When have we seen our family member teach the gospel, either formally or by example?

Discussions and Activities

A. Consider inviting your family member's new Young Women leader to participate in the devotional. Give the leader the opportunity to express her support for your family member and to welcome your family member into Laurels.

B. Display the Young Women Logo and Motto. Near the start of the devotional, ask family members who are, or have been, in Young Women to recite the Young Women theme together.

C. Create a poster listing the Young Women values with their respective colors. Ask family members to name ways in which they've seen the new Laurel demonstrate or cultivate these values. Read Alma 5:14 and discuss the question: How does cultivating these values help a person become more Christlike?

D. Prepare a brief presentation on the Laurel mission statement and symbol. Invite family members—male and female—to testify about how they experience the Savior's love in their lives, or how temple ordinances strengthen them spiritually.

E. Ask each family member to come to the devotional with at least one scripture related to the topic of "faith" or "faithfulness." During the devotional, have family members share these scriptures. Discuss the question: What do we learn from these scriptures about what it means to be a Young Woman of Faith?

F. Obtain or create a list of the kinds of questions asked during a temple recommend interview. Go over the list as a family, discussing things the new Laurel can do over the next two years to ensure her temple readiness.

G. Ask your family member to recount a few of the Value Experiences or Projects she completed as a Mia Maid, focusing especially on experiences in which other family members participated. Then ask your family member to identify the Value Experiences or Projects she still needs to complete in order to receive the Young Womanhood Recognition. Discuss ways in which other family members can support the new Laurel as she continues to work on Personal Progress.

H. From the Young Women Personal Progress booklet, review the list of Value Experiences your family member still needs to complete. Take note of Value Experiences which could be carried out in a family devotional or home evening. Read Mosiah 4:27. Resolve that on a regular, periodic basis, you and your family member will plan a devotional or home evening related to one of the Value Experiences.

I. Give each family member the opportunity to voice their congratulations, hopes, or wishes to the new Laurel.

J. In lieu of a prayer, consider closing with a priesthood blessing for the new Laurel.

Ideas for Individual Instruction

This would be an especially appropriate occasion for an individual discussion with your family member about the on-going challenges and opportunities of adolescence.

A. Read Ecclesiastes 3:1-5 and D&C 64:32. Make a list of experiences which your family member has waited (or is still waiting) to enjoy: driving, dating, working, voting, receiving the endowment, and so on. Discuss the question: Why has your family member been required to wait to experience these things?

Then read Song of Solomon 3:1-4. Explain (1) that sexual desire is not merely a physical appetite, but a longing for intimacy, and (2) that such intimacy requires maturity and the ability to maintain committed relationships.

Together, list the risks—both temporal and spiritual—of adolescent sexual behavior and the blessings that come from waiting until marriage to enter a sexual relationship. Invite your family member to make a personal pledge of abstinence. Discuss ways she can cultivate the spiritual and emotional strength to keep that pledge. A priesthood blessing may be helpful.

B. Point out to your family member that one of the temple ordinances for which she is preparing as a Laurel is eternal marriage. Read Abraham 5:14-18. Share with your family member your concept of the ideal mate, and invite her to do the same.

Explain that dating lets us develop closer friendships with members of the opposite sex, refine our ideas about what we want in a mate, and, ultimately, prepare for courtship. Express your enthusiasm at seeing your family member move into this stage of her life.

Discuss the family rules or guidelines that will apply to your family member's dating. It may be helpful to read together from the pamphlet, *For the Strength of Youth*. Take the time to address questions or concerns your family member may have about beginning to date.

C. Discuss your family member's progress toward high school graduation. What decisions will she need to make over the next two or three years concerning her life after high school? What preparations will she need to undertake (preparing for standardized exams, applying to colleges, seeking scholarships)?

Read D&C 64:33 and Mosiah 4:27. Divide a piece of paper into four columns, one column for each of the next four years. For each year, list major events that will occur in your family member's life or preparations she will need to undertake. Make plans to follow up regularly with your family member to help her meet these demands without becoming overwhelmed.

Conclude the interview with a prayer that God will guide and support your family member during this stressful, but rewarding, phase of her life.

D. Read Psalms 71:1-7 and Alma 37:35-37. Invite your family member to discuss some of the challenges she's faced over the past two years. What has helped her confront those challenges? Commend your family member for ways in which you've seen her develop spiritual strength. Discuss the challenges and major life decisions she will face during the next two years. Express your confidence in her ability to meet those challenges and to make wise choices.

Follow up on your family member's program of personal scripture study and invite her to set new scripture study goals for the coming year. Testify of how prayer and the scriptures help you experience the Savior's love and make major decisions.

Becoming a Deacon

Songs and Hymns

Search, Ponder, and Pray (*Children's Songbook* 109)
I Will Be Valiant (*Children's Songbook* 162)
A Young Man Prepared (*Children's Songbook* 166)
As Zion's Youth in Latter Days (*Hymns* 256)
As I Search the Holy Scriptures (*Hymns* 277)

I Am a Child of God (*Hymns* 301, *Children's Songbook* 2)
Rise Up, O Men of God (*Hymns* 324)

Lesson Ideas
A. The Calling of a Deacon

D&C 20:58-60 (Deacons exhort, teach, and invite all to come to Christ.)

D&C 80:4-5 (Declare the things ye verily believe and know to be true.)

1 Nephi 17:15 (Nephi exhorted his brethren to faithfulness.)

• How can a 12-year-old exhort, teach, and invite others to come to Christ?

• At this stage in his life, what gospel principles is our family member able to bear personal testimony of?

• How will his service as a deacon help him develop his testimony further?

B. Stand for Truth and Righteousness

Matthew 5:16 or *3 Nephi 12:16* (Let your light so shine.)

1 Timothy 4:12 (Be thou an example.)

D&C 115:5 (Be a standard for the nations.)

• When have we seen our family member serve as an example of Christlike behavior?

• As a deacon, what opportunities will he have to share God's light with others?

• How can a 12-year-old stand for truth and righteousness?

C. A Son of God

2 Peter 1:2-8 (Partakers of the divine nature.)

• How will the physical, mental, and social development our family member's experiences during adolescence make him more like our Heavenly Father?

• What divine qualities are listed in this scripture?

• How will service as a deacon help our family member cultivate these qualities?

D. Exercising Accountability

Matthew 25:21 (Thou hast been faithful over a few things.)

Alma 53:20 (The sons of Helaman were true in whatever they were entrusted.)

D&C 58:27-28 (The power is in you to do good.)

• Why is God willing to trust our family member with priesthood responsibilities?

• How will service as a deacon help our family member develop responsibility?

• Why is learning to make our own choices an important part of adolescence?

E. Embarking in God's Service

Matthew 25:34-40 (The parable of the sheep and the goats.)

Mosiah 2:17 (To serve your fellow beings is to serve God.)

D&C 4:1-3 (O ye that embark in the service of God.)

• In what sense is our new deacon embarking in God's service?

• What do we learn from these passages about how to serve God?

• As a deacon, what opportunities will our family member have to serve others?

F. The Mission of the Aaronic Priesthood

Numbers 16:8-9 (Seemeth it a small thing to minister to the congregation?)

2 Chronicles 29:4-7, 11 (The Levites cared for the Lord's house.)

Hebrews 7:5 (The Levites received the people's offerings.)

D&C 107:20 (The Aaronic priesthood administers baptism.)

JS-H 1:68-71 (John the Baptist restored the Aaronic priesthood.)

• What do these passages teach us about the Aaronic priesthood's mission?

• In what ways does a deacon contribute to that mission?

• How can we support our family member in his priesthood responsibilities?

Discussions and Activities

A. Consider inviting the deacons quorum adviser participate in the devotional. Give the adviser the opportunity to express his support for your family member and to welcome your family member into the quorum.

B. Prepare a brief presentation on the purposes of the Aaronic priesthood (see the Aaronic Priesthood guidebook for deacons, p. 7). Discuss the question: How does our family help its members work toward these goals?

C. Using the Aaronic Priesthood guidebook for deacons, explain the Duty to God program to your family. Explain that as a deacon, your family member will complete activities and goals related to his family and priesthood duties and to various areas of his personal development. As a family, you might create a poster-sized version of the "Duty to God Record Sheet" (at the back of the guidebook) to display someplace where family members can see it often.

D. As a family, create a poster, using drawings, photos, pictures from Church magazines, and so on, to depict the calling of a deacon. Include the charge to expound, exhort, teach, and invite all to come to Christ (see D&C 20:59). Following the devotional, hang the poster in the new deacon's room.

E. Read D&C 20:60. Ask each family member to name a gift, quality, or talent they believe the new deacon possesses which will help him magnify his calling.

F. In advance, ask your family member to complete the following sentences. If he wants, he might prepare a collage to represent his answers visually.

- When I picture in my mind who God is, I see . . .
- I believe following Christ means . . .
- What I value about being a member of the Church is . . .
- I believe I'm on earth in order to . . .
- I believe the absolute most important things in life are . . .
- I feel good about myself as a person when . . .

During the devotional, have your family member read his completed sentences, or interpret his collage, to the rest of the family. Point out that what he has just shared is his testimony. Discuss how your family member's experiences as a deacon will help him further develop his testimony of the restored gospel. Also, discuss ways in which your family member can share his testimony with others, in fulfilment of the calling of a deacon.

G. Read 1 Corinthians 12:4-6, 12-18 and D&C 46:10-12. Explain that there are many ways of serving our Heavenly Father's children. Discuss the following questions:

- What kinds of service will our family member render as an Aaronic priesthood holder?
- In what ways do other members of our family serve the Church?

• What kinds of community service do family members provide?
• How does the service rendered by members of our family help to strengthen the body of Christ and make the world a better place?

H. Recall the blessings and admonitions given to other family members when they were ordained to the Aaronic priesthood. Encourage family members to pay attention to what is said during the upcoming ordination. After the ordination, each family member could create a drawing to represent one of the blessings or admonitions given to the new deacon. These drawings could be preserved with the deacon's scrapbook or journal.

I. Family members might present the deacon with gifts that relate to his new calling (a white shirt, a tie, a set of scriptures).

J. Give each family member the opportunity to voice their hopes, wishes, or support to the new (or soon-to-be) deacon.

K. Review the various activities and goals required for the Duty to God certificate for deacons. Take note of activities which could be carried out in a family devotional or home evening. Read Mosiah 4:27. Resolve that on a regular, periodic basis, you and your family member will plan a devotional or home evening related to one of the Duty to God requirements.

Ideas for Individual Instruction

This would be an especially appropriate occasion for an individual discussion with your family member about the challenges and opportunities of adolescence.

A. Read 2 Peter 2:2-4 and paragraph 2 of the Proclamation on the Family ("All human beings—male and female—are created in the image of God. Each is a beloved spirit son or daughter of heavenly parents, and, as such, each has a divine nature and destiny"). Explain that the physical changes which accompany adolescence—including sexual development—make us more like our heavenly parents.

Find out how your family member feels about his physical development. Take the time to answer questions he may have. Let him know how excited you are to see him beginning the transition from childhood to adulthood.

B. Read JS-H 1:28. Discuss the importance of making friends who respect our values and support us in the pursuit of our goals, especially during the adolescent years. Then read Proverbs 17:17 and

2 Nephi 1:30. Together, brainstorm a list of the qualities of a true friend. Help your family member think of ways in which he could demonstrate these qualities in his friendships.

As part of your discussion of friendship, review what the law of chastity teaches us about appropriate relationships. It may be helpful to read together from the pamphlet, *For the Strength of Youth.* Revisit the rules that govern your family member's interaction with friends (for instance, curfews). Make whatever adjustments to the rules seem appropriate to your family member's developing maturity.

C. Read Proverbs 4:13 and D&C 93:36. Find out what aspirations your family member has for his adult life. Discuss the importance of education in helping him pursue his dreams and develop his potential, especially during his adolescent years. Praise your family member for his progress in school. Discuss concerns you or he may have (grades that need improving, the transition into middle school or junior high, and so on).

D. Discuss the exciting opportunities that await your family member during his adolescent years. Then discuss the kinds of hurt, frustration, stress, and insecurity adolescence might bring. Read Psalms 71:1-7 and Alma 37:35-37. Help your family member set up a program of regular personal scripture study and prayer. Testify of the role that prayer and the scriptures play in helping you face challenges and adversity.

Becoming a Teacher

Songs and Hymns
I'm Trying to Be like Jesus (*Children's Songbook* 78)
I Will Be Valiant (*Children's Songbook* 162)
More Holiness Give Me (*Hymns* 131)
Lord, I Would Follow Thee (*Hymns* 220)
Have I Done Any Good? (*Hymns* 223)
As Zion's Youth in Latter Days (*Hymns* 256)
Rise Up, O Men of God (*Hymns* 324)

Lesson Ideas
A. The Calling of a Teacher

D&C 20:53-55 (Teachers strengthen members and prevent backbiting.)

D&C 81:5 (Stand in your office, strengthen the feeble knees.)

Matthew 5:9 or *3 Nephi 12:9* (Blessed are the peacemakers.)

• How can a 14-year-old help strengthen or uplift others?

• How can a 14-year-old act as a peacemaker or encourage kindness?

• When have we seen our family member be a positive influence on others?

B. Stand for Truth and Righteousness

Matthew 5:16 or *3 Nephi 12:16* (Let your light so shine.)

Mosiah 18:9 (Stand as witnesses of God at all times.)

D&C 124:15, 20 (The Lord commended the integrity of early Saints.)

• What situations might a 14-year-old face which require integrity?

• When have we seen our family member stand, by example, as a witness for God?

• As a teacher, what opportunities will he have to share God's light with others?

C. A Son of God

2 Peter 1:2-8 (Partakers of the divine nature.)

1 John 4:7-8 (Every one that loveth knoweth God, for God is love.)

Moroni 7:48 (If we are filled with love, we will be like Christ.)

• When have we seen our family member exhibit the qualities listed in 2 Peter 1:5-7?

• How will service as a teacher help him develop Christlike love?

• Why is it necessary to pray for love?

D. Exercising Accountability

2 Nephi 2:11, 15-16, 27-28 (We are free to act for ourselves.)

• As a 14- or 15-year-old, what new freedoms will our family member enjoy?

• What examples do we see in today's world of teenagers making unwise choices?

• When have we seen our family member exercise responsibility?

E. Persevering in God's Service

D&C 6:8-10 (You shall be the means of doing much good.)

D&C 46:11-12 (Everyone has a spiritual gift.)

D&C 58:27-28 (Be anxiously engaged in a good cause.)

• What talents or gifts has our family member been blessed with?

• When have we seen him using his gifts to serve others?

• As a teacher, what opportunities will he have to do good in the world?

F. The Mission of the Aaronic Priesthood

Numbers 16:8-9 (Seemeth it a small thing to minister to the congregation?)

2 Chronicles 29:4-7, 11 (The Levites cared for the Lord's house.)

Hebrews 7:5 (The Levites received the people's offerings.)

D&C 107:20 (The Aaronic priesthood administers baptism.)

JS-H 1:68-71 (John the Baptist restored the Aaronic priesthood.)

• What do these passages teach us about the Aaronic priesthood's mission?

• In what ways does a teacher contribute to that mission?

• How can we support our family member in his priesthood responsibilities?

Discussions and Activities

A. Consider inviting the teachers quorum adviser to participate in the devotional. Give the adviser the opportunity to express his support for your family member and to welcome your family member into the quorum.

B. Prepare a brief presentation reviewing the purposes of the Aaronic priesthood (see the Aaronic Priesthood guidebook for teachers, p. 7). Discuss the question: How did we see our family member progress towards these goals during his service as a deacon? How will he continue to progress towards these goals as a teacher?

C. Create a graphic showing the four areas of personal development from the Duty to God program (see the Aaronic Priesthood guidebook for teachers, p. 9). Ask family members to identify ways in which they've seen the new (or soon-to-be) teacher develop in each of these areas. Read D&C 93:13 and discuss the question: Why is personal development a lifelong goal for all of us? Preview some of the activities from the Duty to God program which will help your family member continue to develop in the four areas during his time as a teacher.

D. As a family, create a poster, using drawings, photos, pictures from Church magazines, and so on, to depict the calling of a teacher. Include the charge to strengthen Church members and see that there is no hardness, backbiting, or evil speaking (D&C 20:53-54). Following the devotional, hang the poster in the new teacher's room.

E. Read D&C 20:60. Ask each family member to name a gift, quality, or talent they believe the new teacher possesses which will help him magnify his calling. Invite family members to focus especially on talents or qualities which they have seen him cultivate during his time as a deacon.

F. Read Luke 22:32. Discuss the questions: How have we seen our family member's commitment to Christlike living deepen during his time as a deacon? What qualities would we expect to find in a person who has been appointed to strengthen others, as a teacher is called to do (see D&C 20:53)? How can the new teacher cultivate those qualities in his life?

Then read D&C 108:7. Discuss the questions: When have you felt strengthened by someone else? What did the other person do that made you feel that way? Invite the new teacher to set a personal goal to do something in the next two weeks to help someone feel strengthened. Have him report back to the family on his experience.

G. Read Philippians 2:14-15 and 3 Nephi 12:16. Discuss the importance of teaching by example. As a family, brainstorm a list of ways your family member can let his light shine as a teacher.

H. Give each family member the opportunity to voice their hopes, wishes, or support to the new (or soon-to-be) teacher.

I. Review the various activities and goals required for the Duty to God certificate for teachers. Take note of activities which could be carried out in a family devotional or home evening. Read Mosiah 4:27. Resolve that on a regular, periodic basis, you and your family member will plan a devotional or home evening related to one of the Duty to God requirements.

Ideas for Individual Instruction

This would be an especially appropriate occasion for an individual discussion with your family member about the on-going challenges and opportunities of adolescence.

A. Read Psalms 139:14 and Moses 2:27, 31. Point out that many teenagers feel embarrassment or anxiety because of the physical effects of puberty (acne, awkward growth spurts, and so on). Discuss the question: What do these scriptures tell your family member about his body?

Together, make a list of behaviors that abuse the body (drug use, risk-taking, and so on). Discuss the questions: What pressures lead some teenagers to engage in these behaviors? What better ways are there to react to those pressures?

B. Read John 15:12-13. Describe for your family member your notion of an ideal friend, and invite him to do the same. Commend your family member for specific moments in which you've seen him be a supportive friend. Testify about the role that good friends played in helping you face the challenges of adolescence.

As part of your discussion of friendship, review what the law of chastity teaches us about appropriate relationships. It may be helpful to read together from the pamphlet, *For the Strength of Youth*. Revisit the rules that govern your family member's interaction with friends (for instance, curfews). Make whatever adjustments to the rules seem appropriate to your family member's developing maturity.

C. Read D&C 88:118. Commend your family member for specific ways in which you've seen him increase in knowledge, both spiritual and secular, during the last two years. Since your family member will probably enroll in seminary at some point during his years as a teacher, discuss the role of seminary in helping him become a more effective servant of God.

D. Read Psalms 71:1-7 and Alma 37:35-37. Invite your family member to discuss some of the challenges he's faced during the past two years. What has helped him confront those challenges? Commend your family member for ways in which you've seen him develop spiritual strength.

Follow up on your family member's program of personal scripture study and invite him to set new scripture study goals for the coming year. Testify of how a close relationship with God helps you face challenges and adversity.

Becoming a Priest

Songs and Hymns
The Sacrament (*Children's Songbook* 72)
I Love to See the Temple (*Children's Songbook* 95)
I Hope They Call Me on a Mission (*Children's Songbook* 169)
I Will Be Valiant (*Children's Songbook* 162)
'Tis Sweet to Sing the Matchless Love (*Hymns* 177)
As Zion's Youth in Latter Days (*Hymns* 256)
Thy Servants Are Prepared (*Hymns* 261)
Rise Up, O Men of God (*Hymns* 324)

Lesson Ideas
A. The Calling of a Priest
1 Corinthians 11:23-26 (Jesus instituted the sacrament during his ministry.)
3 Nephi 18:1-12 (Jesus instituted the sacrament in the New World.)
D&C 20:46-47 (The duties of a priest.)
• What difference does it make to realize that when a priest blesses the sacrament, he is doing something Jesus himself did?
• By administering the sacrament, how is a priest helping to strengthen members?
• How can a priest carry out the other responsibilities listed in D&C 20:46-47?

B. Stand for Truth and Righteousness
John 13:34 (By this shall all know ye are my disciples.)
Mosiah 18:8-9 (Stand as witnesses of God at all times.)
Alma 5:33-34 (The Lord's arms are extended towards all.)
• How is showing love a way of standing as a witness of God?

• When have we see our family member acting out of love for others?

• What opportunities does a priest have to reach out to others, as the Savior did?

C. A Son of God

Alma 5:11-16, 26-28 (Have ye experienced this mighty change?)

• How have we seen our family member become more Christlike over the last four years?

• When have we seen him bring forth "works of righteousness"?

• How will preparing for a mission and for the temple help him grow spiritually?

D. Exercising Accountability

2 Nephi 32:5 (The Holy Ghost will show you what ye should do.)

Alma 37:37 (Counsel with the Lord in all thy doings.)

D&C 6:14-15 (Thou hast been enlightened by the Spirit.)

• What major life decisions will our family member make during the next 2-3 years?

• How have his experiences as an Aaronic priesthood holder helped prepare him to make those decisions wisely?

• What other resources are available to help him make these decisions?

E. Preach, Teach, Expound, Exhort

D&C 6:8-9 (You shall be the means of doing much good.)

D&C 18:15 (If you bring save it be but one soul to me.)

D&C 88:77 (Teach one another the doctrine of the kingdom.)

• In what sense is doing good a way of "expounding" the gospel?

• What opportunities does a priest have to help bring others closer to God?

• When have we seen our family member teach the gospel, either formally or by example?

F. The Mission of the Aaronic Priesthood

Numbers 16:8-9 (Seemeth it a small thing to minister to the congregation?)

2 Chronicles 29:4-7, 11 (The Levites cared for the Lord's house.)

Hebrews 7:5 (The Levites received the people's offerings.)

D&C 107:20 (The Aaronic priesthood administers baptism.)

JS-H 1:68-71 (John the Baptist restored the Aaronic priesthood.)
- What do these passages teach us about the Aaronic priesthood's mission?
- In what ways does a priest contribute to that mission?
- How can we support our family member in his priesthood responsibilities?

Discussions and Activities

A. Consider inviting the priests quorum adviser to participate in the devotional. Give the adviser the opportunity to express his support for your family member and to welcome your family member into the quorum.

B. Prepare a brief presentation reviewing the purposes of the Aaronic priesthood (see the Aaronic Priesthood guidebook for priests, p. 7). Discuss the question: How did we see our family member progress towards these goals during his service as a teacher? How will he continue to progress towards these goals as a priest?

C. Create a graphic showing the four areas of personal development from the Duty to God program (see the Aaronic Priesthood guidebook for priests, p. 9). Ask family members to identify ways in which they've seen the new (or soon-to-be) priest develop in each of these areas. Read Alma 5:14 and discuss the question: How does development in these four areas help a person become more Christlike? Preview some of the activities from the Duty to God program which will help your family member continue to develop in the four areas during his time as a priest.

D. As a family, create a poster, using drawings, photos, pictures from Church magazines, and so on, to depict the calling of a priest (D&C 20:46-47). Following the devotional, hang the poster in the new priest's room.

E. Encourage family members to be especially attentive the first time the new priest blesses the sacrament. Afterwards, invite family members to write letters to the new priest, sharing their thoughts and feelings about seeing him minister in one of the ways that Jesus himself ministered. (Family members too young to write might instead create drawings of their family member administering the sacrament.)

F. Read D&C 20:60. Ask each family member to name a gift, quality, or talent they believe the new priest possesses which will help him magnify his calling. Invite family members to focus especially on talents or qualities which they have seen him cultivate during his time as a teacher.

G. Read Alma 18:18-22. As a family, make a list of the things that Alma instructed the priests to teach the people. Discuss ways in which a 16-year-old can carry out Alma's charge. How can a 16-year-old promote faith? Prevent contention? Foster unity? Encourage people to make right choices? Share the words of the prophets? Testify of the Savior's love?

Then read Alma 18:26. Discuss the questions: How have we seen our family member "wax strong in the Spirit" over the course of his life? What can he do as a priest to further foster his spirituality? How does living the gospel provide strength to face the challenges and demands of adolescence?

H. Point out that the next major steps in the new priest's spiritual development will be (1) receiving the Melchizedek priesthood, (2) receiving the endowment, and (3) serving a full-time mission. Obtain or create a list of the kinds of questions asked during a worthiness interview. Go over the list as a family, discussing things the new priest can do to ensure that he will be prepared for these next major steps.

I. Give each family member the opportunity to voice their hopes, wishes, or support to the new (or soon-to-be) priest.

J. Review the various activities and goals required for the Duty to God certificate for priests. Take note of activities which could be carried out in a family devotional or home evening. Read Mosiah 4:27. Resolve that on a regular, periodic basis, you and your family member will plan a devotional or home evening related to one of the Duty to God requirements.

Ideas for Individual Instruction

This would be an especially appropriate occasion for an individual discussion with your family member about the on-going challenges and opportunities of adolescence.

A. Read Ecclesiastes 3:1-5 and D&C 64:32. Make a list of experiences which your family member has waited (or is still waiting) to enjoy: driving, dating, working, voting, receiving the endowment, and so on. Discuss the question: Why has your family member been required to wait to experience these things?

Then read Song of Solomon 4:8-11. Explain (1) that sexual desire is not merely a physical appetite, but a longing for intimacy, and (2) that such intimacy requires maturity and the ability to maintain committed relationships.

Together, list the risks—both temporal and spiritual—of adolescent sexual behavior and the blessings that come from waiting until marriage to enter a sexual relationship. Invite your family member to make a personal pledge of abstinence. Discuss ways he can cultivate the spiritual and emotional strength to keep that pledge. A priesthood blessing may be helpful.

B. Review the purposes of the Aaronic priesthood as laid out in the Aaronic Priesthood guidebook for priests (p. 7). Point out that one of the purposes of Aaronic priesthood service is to prepare your family member for marriage. Read Abraham 5:14-18. Share with your family member your concept of the ideal mate, and invite him to do the same.

Explain that dating lets us develop closer friendships with members of the opposite sex, refine our ideas about what we want in a mate, and, ultimately, prepare for courtship. Express your enthusiasm at seeing your family member move into this stage of his life.

Discuss the family rules or guidelines that will apply to your family member's dating. It may be helpful to read together from the pamphlet, *For the Strength of Youth*. Take the time to address questions or concerns your family member may have about beginning to date.

C. Discuss your family member's progress towards high school graduation. What decisions will he need to make over the next two or three years concerning his life after high school? What preparations will he need to undertake (preparing for standardized exams, applying to colleges, seeking scholarships)?

Read D&C 64:33 and Mosiah 4:27. Divide a piece of paper into four columns, one column for each of the next four years. For each year, list major events that will occur in your family member's life or preparations that he will need to undertake. Make plans to follow up regularly with your family member to help him meet these demands without becoming overwhelmed.

Conclude the interview with a prayer that God will guide and support your family member during this stressful, but rewarding, phase of his life.

D. Read Psalms 71:1-7 and Alma 37:35-37. Invite your family member to discuss some of the challenges he's faced during the past two years. What has helped him confront those challenges? Commend your family member for ways in which you've seen him develop spiritual strength. Discuss the challenges and major life decisions he will face during the next two years. Express your confidence in his ability to meet those challenges and to make wise choices.

Follow up on your family member's program of personal scripture study and invite him to set new scripture study goals for the coming year. Testify of how prayer and the scriptures provide you with spiritual strength and help you make major decisions.

Patriarchal Blessing

Songs and Hymns
I Will Follow God's Plan (*Children's Songbook* 164)
Tell Me, Dear Lord (*Children's Songbook* 176)
Lead, Kindly Light (*Hymns* 97)
Guide Me to Thee (*Hymns* 101)
Jesus, Savior, Pilot Me (*Hymns* 104)
Be Thou Humble (*Hymns* 130)
I Am a Child of God (*Hymns* 301, *Children's Songbook* 2)

Lesson Ideas
A. Blessings Are an Ancient Custom
Genesis 24:60-62 (Rebekah's family blessed her before she left home.)

Genesis 28:1-4 (Jacob was blessed by Isaac before leaving home.)

Numbers 6:22-27 (Aaron and his sons blessed the people of Israel.)

Alma 35:15-16 (Alma gave each of his sons a charge.)

• What do these passages tell us about the purpose of blessings in ancient times?

- What is meant by a "charge" (Alma 35:16; see also Genesis 28:1)?
- How do patriarchal blessings continue this ancient practice in modern times?

B. Seeking God's Counsel

Psalms 25:4-5 (Shew me thy ways, O Lord; teach me thy paths.)

Psalms 143:7-8 (Cause me to know the way wherein I should walk.)

Alma 37:37 (Counsel with the Lord, and he will direct thee for good.)

- What difference does it make to know that God will counsel us individually?
- How does receiving a patriarchal blessing show a desire to receive God's counsel?
- What various means might God use to direct or teach us?

C. Line upon Line

Colossians 1:9-11 (May you be filled with knowledge of God's will.)

2 Nephi 28:30 (I will give line upon line, precept upon precept.)

D&C 78:17-18 (Ye have not yet understood, but I will lead you along.)

- Why does our understanding of God's will for each of us unfold only gradually?
- How does a patriarchal blessing contribute to the on-going process of personal revelation?
- What other aids to personal revelation are available to us?

D. Using God's Gifts to Us

1 Corinthians 12:4-11 (There is a diversity of spiritual gifts.)

Alma 37:14-17 (God has entrusted you with sacred things.)

D&C 6:8-10 (You shall be the means of doing much good.)

- What different gifts or capabilities do we see in the members of our family?
- How do these gifts equip family members to serve God and others?
- What can a patriarchal blessing teach us about how God wants us to use our gifts?

E. God's Promises Will Be Fulfilled

2 Peter 1:2-4 (We have been given exceeding great promises.)

D&C 3:1-3 (The purposes of God cannot be frustrated.)

D&C 88:63-64, 68 (God fulfills his promises in his own time and way.)

- What kinds of promises does a patriarchal blessing typically contain?

- In what sense is a patriarchal blessing an individual reaffirmation of promises already made to all of God's children?

- What difference does it make to know that we each have these promises from God?

Discussions and Activities

A. Family members who have already received their patriarchal blessings might judge it appropriate to describe how promises made in their patriarchal blessings have given them assurance and direction in life.

B. As a family, make a list of some of the major life decisions that confront the family member who is preparing to receive his/her patriarchal blessing. Once the family member has received a written copy of the blessing, invite him/her to conduct a follow-up lesson, sharing with the family how the patriarchal blessing helped to cast light on the decisions on the list. Discuss what other means the family member might use to obtain counsel and personal revelation.

C. Give family members the opportunity to express their hopes or wishes on behalf of the person who is preparing to receive his/her patriarchal blessing.

D. If the whole family will be present during the blessing, encourage family members to be attentive to what is said. Afterwards, each family member could create a drawing to represent one of the blessings or admonitions bestowed by the patriarch. Present these drawings to the person who received the blessing, as a keepsake.

E. Encourage the family member who is preparing to receive his/her patriarchal blessing to spend time reflecting (perhaps in his/her journal) on questions such as these:

- What do I know so far about God's plan for me?
- How do I feel God wants me to use my gifts?
- What do I sense God may be inspiring me to do with my life?

• What do I still need to discover about my mission on earth?

F. Encourage family members who have received their patriarchal blessings to set aside a time to reread their blessings and to record in their journals their latest insights. Encourage family members who have not received their patriarchal blessings to reflect in their journals on their on-going preparation to receive a patriarchal blessing.

G. Family members might consider fasting with the person who is preparing to receive his/her patriarchal blessing.

Entering the Relief Society

Songs and Hymns
I'm Trying to Be like Jesus (*Children's Songbook* 78)
I Want to Live the Gospel (*Children's Songbook* 148)
Because I Have Been Given Much (*Hymns* 219)
Lord, I Would Follow Thee (*Hymns* 220)
Love One Another (*Hymns* 308, *Children's Songbook* 136)
As Sisters in Zion (*Hymns* 309)
A Key Was Turned in Latter Days (*Hymns* 310)

Lesson Ideas
A. The Mission of the Relief Society
Colossians 3:12-17 (Put on charity, teach one another, do all things in the Lord's name.)
Mosiah 4:26-27 (Administer to the relief of the poor.)
D&C 82:14 (Zion must arise and put on her beautiful garments.)
• How do these passages relate to the Relief Society's mission?
• How have her experiences in Young Women prepared our family member to help carry out the Relief Society's mission?
• In what ways will she be blessed by active membership in the Relief Society?

B. Charity Never Faileth
1 Corinthians 13:1-8 (Charity never faileth)
Moroni 7:47-48 (Charity is the pure love of Christ.)
D&C 88:125 (Above all things, clothe yourselves with charity.)

- What does it mean to say, "Charity never faileth"?
- When have we seen our family member demonstrate the qualities of charity?
- How does the Relief Society serve as a vehicle for rendering Christlike service?

C. Handmaid of the Lord

Luke 1:26-38, 46-49 (Mary accepted God's mission for her.)
- What "great things" (v. 49) has God done for our family member?
- In what sense does our family member, like Mary, have a mission to fulfill in life?
- How can activity in the Relief Society help her carry out that mission?

D. Moving into Adulthood

Joshua 1:8-9 (God is with thee whithersoever thou goest.)
2 Nephi 31:12 (Do the things which ye have seen me do.)
D&C 58:27 (Be anxiously engaged in a good cause.)
- What counsel do these passages offer to someone moving into adulthood?
- How have we seen our family member mature and become more Christlike during her adolescent years?
- What opportunities for service will she have as a member of the Relief Society?

E. Building up God's Kingdom

Luke 12:29-34 (Seek the kingdom of God, not earthly treasures.)
Jacob 2:18-19 (Before ye seek for riches, seek for the kingdom of God.)
D&C 15:4, 6 (The thing of most worth to you is to bring souls to me.)
- How do members of the Relief Society help to build up God's kingdom?
- Why is this phase of her life an especially important time for our family member to commit to use her means to serve God and others?
- As a member of the Relief Society, how can she help others draw closer to God?

Discussions and Activities

A. As a family, create a poster bearing the Relief Society seal. Underneath the seal, ask each family member to write a sentence, summarizing what the slogan "Charity Never Faileth" means to him/her.

B. Display a copy of the Relief Society Declaration. Invite family members—male and female—to testify about any of the following:

• How the gospel gives their lives "meaning, purpose, and direction."

• How prayer and scripture study have strengthened their testimonies of the Savior.

• How they strive to develop their full potential as children of God.

• The practices that bring them spiritual strength.

• The importance of supportive, nurturing family relationships.

• The satisfaction that comes from serving others.

• The role of priesthood ordinances, including temple ordinances, in their lives.

• Ways they have seen the new Relief Society member show love for life.

• Ways they have seen her stand for truth and righteousness.

C. Ask each family member to come to the devotional with at least one scriptural passage which describes something Jesus or his apostles did to build God's kingdom or help others. Discuss the question: In what ways does the Relief Society continue the work of Jesus and his apostles in modern times? As a family, create a poster or collage with the slogan, "Ye are called to the work" (D&C 4:3) and present it to the new Relief Society member.

D. Read D&C 6:10. Discuss the question: What gifts, or talents, or qualities does our family member bring with her to the Relief Society?

E. Ask a family member—preferably one who is a member of the Relief Society—to recount the story of how the Relief Society was founded. Discuss the question: How does the Relief Society in modern times continue to carry out its original mission?

F. Ask family members to prepare brief presentations on women from the scriptures who exemplify faith, virtue, vision, or charity. These include:

- *Eve:* set in motion the plan of happiness (Moses 4:7-12; 5:11).
- *Sarah:* entered into the Lord's covenant (Genesis 17:15-16).
- *Rebekah:* received personal revelation (Genesis 25:21-23).
- *Miriam:* a leader of the women of Israel (Exodus 15:20-21).
- *Ruth:* left her country to care for her widowed mother-in-law (Ruth 1).
- *Deborah:* served as a judge over Israel (Judges 4).
- *Hannah:* prayed for the Lord's help in her troubles (1 Samuel 1).
- *The wise woman of Tekoah:* served as a peacemaker (2 Samuel 14:1-20).
- *The widow of Zarephath:* trusted in God's power (1 Kings 8:16).
- *Huldah:* exhorted king Josiah to keep the covenant (2 Chronicles 34).
- *Esther:* risked her life in order to save her people (Esther 4).
- *Mary of Nazareth:* accepted God's mission for her (Luke 1:26-38).
- *Elizabeth:* received discernment from the Spirit (Luke 1:39-45).
- *Ana:* served God in the temple (Luke 2:36-38).
- *The Samaritan woman:* told her neighbors about Christ (John 4).
- *The widow in the temple:* gave everything she had (Mark 12:41-44).
- *Martha:* received the Lord into her home (Luke 10:38).
- *Mary of Bethany:* sought spiritual knowledge (Luke 10:39-42).
- *Mary Magdalene:* testified of the risen Lord (John 20:1-18).
- *Tabitha (Dorcas):* known for her good works (Acts. 9:36-42).
- *Priscilla:* an early missionary (Acts 18; Romans 16:3-4).
- *Phebe:* a servant of the church and a succourer of many (Romans 16:1-2).
- *Sarai:* left her home to fulfill God's will (1 Nephi 2).
- *The Lamanite queen:* commended for her faith (Alma 19:2-10).
- *Abish:* instrumental in bringing the gospel to the Lamanites (Alma 19).

• *The Ammonite mothers:* taught their children to trust God (Alma 56:45-48).

• *Emma Smith:* called to assist in the work of the Restoration (D&C 25).

• *Vienna Jacques:* called by the Lord to help build Zion (D&C 90:28-31).

G. If other members of the family already belong to the Relief Society, they could extend a formal welcome to the new member. For instance, they could present her with a copy of the Declaration of the Relief Society, the Relief Society seal, or the study guide for that year.

H. Give each family member the opportunity to express their congratulations, hopes, or wishes on behalf of the new Relief Society member.

I. Entering the Relief Society is part of a young LDS woman's transition into adulthood. This might be a good opportunity to discuss the challenges that transition brings, both for the young woman herself (for instance, going away to school) and for other members of the family (for instance, learning to untie the apron strings). The story of Rebekah leaving her family (Genesis 24) might provide a scriptural opening for this discussion.

J. In lieu of a prayer, consider closing the devotional with a priesthood blessing for the new Relief Society member.

Receiving the Melchizedek Priesthood

Songs and Hymns

I'm Trying to Be like Jesus (*Children's Songbook* 78)
I Want to Live the Gospel (*Children's Songbook* 148)
Lord, I Would Follow Thee (*Hymns* 220)
Thy Servants Are Prepared (*Hymns* 261)
Ye Elders of Israel (*Hymns* 319)
Rise Up, O Men of God (*Hymns* 324)
Brightly Beams Our Father's Mercy (*Hymns* 335)

Lesson Ideas

A. The Mission of the Melchizedek Priesthood

Genesis 14:18-20 (Melchizedek blessed Abraham and received his tithes)

John 21:15-17 (Jesus charged Peter to feed his sheep.)

D&C 27:12-13 (The Melchizedek priesthood continues the work of Jesus' apostles.)

D&C 84:19-21 (Through the Melchizedek priesthood, God's power is manifest.)

• What do these passages teach us about the Melchizedek priesthood's mission?

• In what ways does an elder contribute to that mission?

• How can we support our family member in his priesthood responsibilities?

B. The Calling of an Elder

1 Peter 5:1-3 (Peter charged the elders to feed the flock and be examples.)

Alma 6:1 (Alma ordained elders to watch over the church.)

D&C 133:8-9 (The elders are sent to the nations to build up Zion.)

• When have we seen our family member serve as an example of Christlike living?

• As an elder, how will our family member help nourish other church members?

• How is our family member preparing himself for missionary service?

C. Ordained to Be a Servant

Matthew 24:45-51 or *JS-M 1:49-54* (Faithful and unfaithful servants.)

Luke 22:24-27 (To hold Christ's authority is to serve.)

D&C 121:34-46 (Priesthood holders are warned against unrighteous dominion.)

• What do we learn from these passages about the qualities of a faithful servant?

• When have we seen our family member serve others as Jesus served?

• In what ways might a Melchizedek priesthood holder be tempt-
ed to exercise unrighteous dominion?

D. Moving into Adulthood

1 Corinthians 16:13-14 (Quit ye like men; do all things with charity.)

3 Nephi 27:27 (What manner of men ought ye to be? Even as I
am.)

D&C 58:27 (Be anxiously engaged in a good cause.)

• How have we seen our family member mature during his adolescent years?

• How have we seen him become more Christlike or charitable?

• What opportunities for service will he have as a Melchizedek
priesthood holder?

E. Building up God's Kingdom

Luke 12:29-34 (Seek the kingdom of God, not earthly treasures.)

Jacob 2:18-19 (Before ye seek for riches, seek for the kingdom of
God.)

D&C 15:4, 6 (The thing of most worth to you is to bring souls to
me.)

• How does receiving the Melchizedek priesthood entail a commitment to use one's means to serve God and others?

• Why is this phase of his life an especially important time for our
family member to make that commitment?

• How will missionary service bless our family member as he
enters adulthood?

Discussions and Activities

A. Ask each family member to come to the devotional with at
least one scriptural passage which describes something Jesus or his
apostles did to build God's kingdom or help others. Discuss the question: In what ways does an elder continue the work of Jesus and his
apostles in modern times? As a family, create a poster or collage with
the slogan, "Jesus Christ hath called you to his ministry" (Moroni
8:2) and present it to the new (or soon-to-be) elder.

B. Point out that your family member is about to do what in other
denominations would be called "entering the priesthood" or "entering the ministry." Invite your family member to share his feelings

about the commitment to service he is taking upon himself. In what practical ways does this commitment affect his life? How does it influence his sense of who he is and what he hopes to accomplish as an adult?

C. Read Alma 4:6-8. Discuss the questions: What can an 18- or 19-year-old elder do to combat materialism? What can he do to promote better relations between Latter-day Saints and members of other faiths?

D. Read D&C 20:60. Ask each family member to identify a gift, talent, or quality they believe the new elder brings to his service as a Melchizedek priesthood holder.

E. Read 1 Corinthians 12:4-6, 12-18 and D&C 46:10-12. Explain that there are many ways of serving our Heavenly Father's children. Discuss the following questions:

• What kinds of service will our family member render as a Melchizedek priesthood holder?

• In what ways do other members of our family provide service, both in the Church and in the world at large?

• How does the service rendered by members of our family help to strengthen the body of Christ and make the world a better place?

F. Encourage family members to be attentive during the upcoming ordination. Following the ordination, each family member might create a drawing to represent one of the blessings and admonitions the new elder received. Present these drawings to the new elder as a keepsake.

G. Give each family member the opportunity to express their hopes, wishes, or support to the new elder.

H. Melchizedek priesthood ordination is a major step in a young LDS man's transition into adulthood. This might be a good opportunity to discuss the challenges that transition brings, both for the young man himself (for instance, leaving home) and for other members of the family (for instance, learning to untie the apron strings). 1 Corinthians 13:11 could provide a scriptural basis for this discussion.

Receiving the Endowment

Songs and Hymns

I Love to See the Temple (*Children's Songbook* 95)
I Pledge Myself to Love the Right (*Children's Songbook* 161)
"Give," Said the Little Stream (*Children's Songbook* 236)
Lead Me into Life Eternal (*Hymns* 45)
Because I Have Been Given Much (*Hymns* 219)
Rise, Ye Saints, and Temples Enter (*Hymns* 286)
Rejoice, Ye Saints of Latter Days (*Hymns* 290)

Lesson Ideas

A. The Purpose of Temple Worship

1 Kings 8:12-23, 26-30, 54-61 (The dedicatory prayer for Solomon's temple.)

D&C 97:10-16 (The command to build a temple in Zion.)

D&C 109:1-2, 10-23 (The dedicatory prayer for the Kirtland temple.)

• What do we learn from these passages about the purpose of temple worship?

• How has temple worship blessed the lives of members of our family?

• How does temple worship help us carry out God's work (see D&C 109:22-23)?

B. A Covenant to Serve

2 Chronicles 34:29-33 (The people made a covenant in the temple.)

D&C 101:39 (Those who make covenants are the salt of the earth.)

Matthew 5:13-16 or *3 Nephi 12:13-16* (Ye are the salt of the earth.)

• What does it mean to be the salt of the earth?

• How have temple covenants inspired members of our family to serve God and others?

• Why is a covenant commitment to service an important part of the transition into adult life?

C. Consecrating Ourselves to God

Romans 12:1-2 (Present yourselves as a living sacrifice.)
Omni 1:26 (Offer your whole souls unto God.)
Mosiah 2:34 (Render to God all that you have and are.)
• What offerings of time, talents, or means does our family make to God's service?
• How does making those offerings fulfill temple covenants?
• What talents does our family member have that he/she can consecrate to God?

D. Progressing from Grace to Grace

1 John 2:24-25 (Let that abide in you which ye have heard from the beginning.)
2 Nephi 31:19-20 (Press forward with steadfastness in Christ.)
D&C 93:11-20 (Continue from grace to grace, as did the Savior.)
• In what sense is the endowment a reaffirmation of the baptismal covenant?
• How does receiving the endowment help us press forward in Christ?
• How will receiving the endowment aid our family member in his/her on-going spiritual development?

E. Receiving Sacred Instruction

Isaiah 2:2-5 or *2 Nephi 12:2-4* (God will teach us in the temple.)
D&C 97:12-14 (The temple is a place of instruction.)
• In general terms, what kind of instruction do we receive in the temple?
• In what sense does the endowment remind us of truths we already knew?
• What does temple worship teach us about how we should live?

Discussions and Activities

A. Invite family members who have already been to the temple to testify of the peace and inspiration they have experienced there.

B. Invite family members who have received the endowment to relate experiences in which the knowledge that they had made temple covenants afforded them strength or direction in life.

C. Read the dedicatory prayer for the temple which serves your area. Identify the blessings which are promised to those who participate in temple worship. Discuss ways in which you see those promises fulfilled in the lives of family members.

D. As a family, create a poster depicting our eternal progress as a winding path (or perhaps a circle) with the following stations:

    1. Heavenly Father sent us to earth to learn from experience.

    2. The Savior and his messengers teach us God's plan.

    3. Satan tries to lead us astray.

    4. Temple ordinances make it possible for us to return to God.

Illustrate the poster with drawings, family photos, pictures from Church magazines, passages from the scriptures, and so on.

E. Read Numbers 6:1-5. Explain that in cultures throughout the world, there are individuals who, like the Nazarites described in the Old Testament, opt to live by special vows. These individuals adopt distinctive customs, including dress and grooming styles, which make them stand out from other members of their societies. In a similar fashion, those who receive the endowment commit to live by special vows.

Discuss the distinctive lifestyle and dress requirements that your family member will assume when he/she receives the endowment. Ask your family member to explain why he/she is willing to adopt this distinctive lifestyle.

F. Give the family member who is preparing to receive the endowment an opportunity to express his/her feelings about the upcoming experience.

G. Give each family member the opportunity to express their congratulations, hopes, and wishes on behalf of the person who is about to receive the endowment.

H. Encourage your family member to record his/her feelings about the temple experience soon after receiving the endowment. Encourage family members who have already received the endowment to reflect in their journals on the importance of temple covenants in their lives. Encourage other family members to reflect on their preparation to someday attend the temple.

I. During the closing prayer, ask for the following:

• That the family member will have a positive experience in the temple.

• That through receiving the endowment, the family member will gain insight about God's plan for him/her.

• That the Spirit will give the family member power to keep his/her temple covenants and thus be an agent of good in the world.

Ideas for Individual Instruction

The key to a positive first temple experience is preparation. While we are enjoined not to describe certain particulars of sacred rites outside sacred precincts, there is much we can do to prepare family members to understand the symbols employed in the endowment, using the scriptures and other materials produced by the Church.

The lesson ideas and the discussions and activities listed above are designed for use with the entire family. By contrast, the ideas which appear below are meant to be used for one-on-one instruction with the individual who is about to receive the endowment.

If you plan to use more than one of these ideas, consider doing so over a period of a few weeks, to avoid overwhelming your family member with information.

A. Read Exodus 29:1, 4-9 and Revelation 1:4-6. Explain that the endowment draws on priesthood symbols from ancient times. These symbols remind us that we, like the priests of Israel, are called to serve God and our fellow beings and are invited to enter God's presence. Encourage your family member to watch during the endowment for echoes of the rites described in Exodus 29.

B. Read D&C 88:74-75. Discuss the question: What do we see in the world around us that could be thought of as the sins of our generation? Explain that the endowment begins with an initiatory rite that will symbolically cleanse your family member of those sins. (See "Temple Ordinances," Encyclopedia of Mormonism, vol. 4, p. 1444.) Encourage your family member to be attentive to the blessings pronounced upon him/her in the course of the initiatory.

C. Read Revelation 3:4-5 and 2 Nephi 9:14. Note that white clothing is used in the scriptures as a symbol of purity. Explain that during the endowment, your family member will be clothed for the first time in the temple garment, which serves as a constant reminder of our temple covenants. (See "Garments," Encyclopedia of Mormonism, vol. 2, p. 534.) Take this opportunity to answer questions your family member may have about wearing and caring for the garment.

D. Read and discuss the following statement by Brigham Young:

Your endowment is, to receive all those ordinances in the house of the Lord, which are necessary for you, after you have departed this life, to enable you to walk back to the presence of the Father, passing the angels who stand as sentinels, being enabled to give them the key words, the signs and tokens, pertaining to the holy Priesthood, and gain your eternal exaltation in spite of earth and hell. (Discourses of Brigham Young, p. 416).

E. Read or retell Lehi's vision of the tree of life (1 Nephi 8). Then discuss what the various symbols in the vision mean (see 1 Nephi 11-12). Explain that just as Lehi was taught about the plan of salvation through a symbolic drama, so the endowment consists of a symbolic drama which teaches why we are on earth and how we can return to God's presence. (See "Endowments," Encyclopedia of Mormonism, vol. 2, p. 454; also, "Temple Ordinances," Encyclopedia of Mormonism, vol. 4, p. 1444.)

Note that one of the advantages of teaching through symbols is that the same symbol can be applied to a variety of circumstances. Assure your family member that an appreciation of the symbolism of the endowment unfolds gradually. Encourage your family member to apply the counsel of Nephi: to liken the endowment to his/her own life (1 Nephi 19:23).

F. Read 1 Nephi 20:16 ("I have not spoken in secret; from the beginning, from the time that it was declared, have I spoken"). Explain that the endowment doesn't so much present new information as it reinforces truths we have already learned. Following his/her first temple experience, encourage your family member to spend time reflecting on how the endowment reinforces principles such as these:

• Our Heavenly Father loves us and is concerned for our well-being.

• Jesus Christ is Lord and our Mediator with the Father.

• Our life on earth is part of an overarching divine plan.

• Adversity and error are necessary aspects of our eternal development.

• The scriptures, prophets, and apostles teach us how to live.

- The Savior makes it possible for us to return to God's presence.
- Satan exercises great influence in the world but will be defeated.
  - We are called to serve God with all our means and energies.

G. A priesthood blessing for your family member on the eve of his/her receiving the endowment might be helpful.

Missionary Farewell

Songs and Hymns
We'll Bring the World His Truth (*Children's Songbook* 172)
I Need Thee Every Hour (*Hymns* 98)
Cast Thy Burden upon the Lord (*Hymns* 110)
When Faith Endures (*Hymns* 128)
Where Can I Turn For Peace? (*Hymns* 129)
God Be with You Till We Meet Again (*Hymns* 152)
Dear to the Heart of the Shepherd (*Hymns* 221)
Called to Serve (*Hymns* 249, *Children's Songbook* 174)
I'll Go Where You Want Me to Go (*Hymns* 270)

Lesson Ideas
A. Feed My Sheep
John 21:15-17 (Feed my sheep.)
1 Thessalonians 2:4-8 (We were as a nurse who cherisheth her children.)
D&C 12:7-8 (No one can assist in this work without love.)
D&C 81:5 (Succor the weak; strengthen the feeble knees.)
- In what ways will our family member, as a missionary, help nourish others?
- What would a missionary be like who served with faith and diligence, but not love?
- Why is it important for missionaries to be gentle (1 Thessalonians 2:7) and temperate (D&C 12:8)?

B. Be Patient in Affliction
Alma 17:5, 10-11 (Be patient in afflictions.)

Romans 8:28, 31, 35, 37-39 (Nothing can separate us from Christ's love.)

2 Corinthians 4:6-10 (We are troubled, but not in despair.)

• What kinds of adversity can our family member expect to face as a missionary?

• What difference does it make to know that God's love is always with us?

• What does Paul mean when he says that those who suffer adversity in Christ's service bear in their own bodies the dying of the Lord Jesus (2 Corinthians 4:10)?

C. Do Not Fear

Matthew 28:19-20 (I am with you always.)

2 Nephi 7:7 (The Lord will help me; I shall not be ashamed.)

D&C 68:5-6 (Do not fear, for I am with you.)

• What anxieties or worries does our family member have about missionary service?

• What difference does it make to know that the Savior is with our family member?

• How can a missionary's setting apart serve as a source of assurance?

D. Let Your Light Shine

Moses 6:31-32 (Enoch's call to prophesy.)

Isaiah 6:1-8 (Isaiah's call to prophesy.)

Jeremiah 1:6-9 (Jeremiah's call to prophesy.)

Matthew 5:13-16 or *3 Nephi 12:13-16* (Let your light shine.)

• Why did Enoch, Isaiah, and Jeremiah feel inadequate to serve?

• What worries does our family member have about his/her ability to serve?

• What gifts or strengths does our family member take into the mission field?

E. Building up Zion

1 Nephi 13:37 (Blessed are they who seek to bring forth Zion.)

D&C 6:6-8 (You shall be the means of doing much good.)

Moses 7:18 (Why the Lord called his people Zion.)

• As a missionary, how will our family member help build Zion?

• What blessings come from missionary service?

• How do missionaries help make the world better?

F. Supporting Our Missionary

Ephesians 3:14-21 (The Father grant that you be strengthened.)

Moroni 8:2-3 (I am mindful of you always.)

D&C 108:7 (Strengthen your brethren in all your doings.)

• What blessings did Paul and Mormon ask for in their prayers?

• In our prayers, what blessings can we ask for our missionary family member?

• How else can we strengthen our family member in the mission field?

Discussions and Activities

A. Ask family members who have served missions to share experiences related to the chosen theme of the devotional. These same family members might consider writing special letters of encouragement and counsel to the new missionary, to be read once he/she has entered the MTC or the mission field.

B. In the spirit of D&C 93:53, assign family members to research the place where your family member will serve his/her mission. Family members could create presentations on different topics:

• The general history of the area.

• The history of the Church in the area.

• Points of common belief with the dominant religion(s).

• Current social or political concerns.

• Distinctive values, customs, or holiday celebrations.

Discuss how the teachings of the restored gospel could benefit the people of this area, given their particular concerns, struggles, and aspirations.

C. Ask the new missionary to talk about why he/she decided to serve a mission. What experiences solidified the desire to serve, or confirmed that God wanted him/her to serve? What gifts does he/she bring to the mission? What blessings does he/she hope to reap?

D. Give each family member the opportunity to express their congratulations, hopes, or wishes on behalf of the new missionary.

E. Create a poster with the slogan, "We are mindful of you always" (see Moroni 8:3). Place on the poster the new missionary's photo. Ask the missionary to send additional photos to be added to the poster in the course of his/her time away from home.

F. As a gesture of support, each family member could present the new missionary with an item he/she can use in the mission (clothing, toiletries, stationary, and so on).

G. If the whole family will attend the setting apart, encourage family members to be attentive to what is said. Afterwards, family members could create drawings to represent the blessings and admonitions bestowed during the setting apart. These could be turned into a booklet for the new missionary to take into the field for remembrance.

H. If this devotional is being held in advance of the sacrament meeting farewell, this might be a good time to discuss how different family members will contribute to that meeting.

I. Before offering the closing prayer, ask the new (or soon-to-be) missionary what prayers he/she feels in need of.

Missionary Homecoming

Songs and Hymns

For Thy Bounteous Blessings (*Children's Songbook* 21)
I Hope They Call Me on a Mission (*Children's Songbook* 169)
A Mighty Fortress Is Our God (*Hymns* 68)
Press Forward, Saints (*Hymns* 81)
Now Thank We All Our God (*Hymns* 95)
Savior, Redeemer of My Soul (*Hymns* 112)
Count Your Blessings (*Hymns* 241)
Put Your Shoulder to the Wheel (*Hymns* 252)

Lesson Ideas

A. Well Done, Faithful Servant

Matthew 25:14-30 (The parable of the talents.)

• Why did the servant who produced 2 talents receive the same commendation as the servant who produced 5 talents?

• How did our family member magnify his/her calling as a missionary?

• What blessings has our family member seen as a result of his/her service?

B. Disappointments and Regrets

Isaiah 53:1-3 (He is rejected, a man of sorrows.)
Matthew 23:37 (Jesus lamented that he was rejected.)
Alma 8:14-15 (The angel bid Alma rejoice despite his rejection.)
• What disappointments does our family member bring home from the mission?
• What difference does it make to realize that Jesus also knew disappointment?
• What reasons does our family member have to rejoice?

C. Praise and Thanksgiving

1 Thessalonians 2:13 (We thank God because ye received the word.)
Alma 26:8-12 (Blessed be the name of our God.)
Alma 29:9-10 (I remember what the Lord has done for me.)
• What reasons does our returned missionary have to give thanks to God?
• In what ways has our whole family been enriched by the returned missionary's service?
• How can we demonstrate our gratitude for these blessings?

D. Dear unto Us

1 Thessalonians 2:4-9 (Ye were dear unto us.)
2 Timothy 1:1-4 (I have remembrance of thee in my prayers.)
Moroni 8:25-26 (Perfect love endures until the end shall come.)
• How has our family member come to love those he/she served?
• How have these people become dear to our whole family?
• In what ways will we remain mindful of these people?

E. Moving On

Psalms 142:5-8 (Cause me to know the way I should walk.)
2 Nephi 31:19-20 (Press forward with steadfastness in Christ.)
D&C 58:26-28 (Be anxiously engaged in a good cause.)
• What lies ahead for our newly returned missionary?
• How can we help our family member adjust to post-mission life?
• In what ways will our family member continue to serve God and others?

Discussions and Activities

A. Recount back to your family member events from his/her mission which you have remembered. Explain why these events from your family member's mission were significant to you.

B. Give the returned missionary an opportunity to thank each member of the family for the support they provided during his/her mission. The missionary might consider doing this in the form of a letter or note to each family member.

C. As a family, create a poster with the slogan, "We remember what the Lord has done for [family member's name]" (see Alma 29:10). Include mission photos, pictures from Church magazines, drawings, notes, and so on, that illustrate positive experiences or blessings which grew out of the family member's missionary service.

D. As a family, compile a list of (1) blessings experienced by the returned missionary in the course of his/her service, and (2) ways in which the returned missionary's service was a blessing for other family members. Offer a family prayer thanking God for these blessings.

E. As a family, compile a list of individuals the returned missionary worked with who were not baptized (or reactivated, etc.). Offer a family prayer on behalf of those individuals, asking that God will continue to bless and guide them.

F. Encourage the returned missionary to reflect in his/her journal on the direction his/her life will take now that the mission has been completed. Encourage other family members who have served missions to reflect on how their mission experiences continue to influence their lives. Encourage family members who have not yet served missions to reflect on their preparation for missionary service.

G. This might be an appropriate time to discuss adjustments in the household occasioned by the family member's return. Since everyone has changed in the course of the last 18 months or 2 years, it may take a little time to reforge relationships among family members, and there may be some awkwardness or tension.

H. In lieu of a closing prayer, consider concluding the devotional with a priesthood blessing to help the returned missionary make the adjustment to post-mission life.

Marriage

Songs and Hymns

Where Love Is (*Children's Songbook* 138)
Love Is Spoken Here (*Children's Songbook* 190)
The Wise Man and the Foolish Man (*Children's Songbook* 281)
Let Us Oft Speak Kind Words (*Hymns* 232)
Love at Home (*Hymns* 294)
Home Can Be a Heaven on Earth (*Hymns* 298)
Families Can Be Together Forever (*Hymns* 300, *Children's Songbook* 188)
Love One Another (*Hymns* 308, *Children's Songbook* 136)

Lesson Ideas

A. Becoming One Flesh

Genesis 2:18-24 or *Moses 3:18-24* or *Abraham 5:14-18* (They shall be one flesh.)

1 Corinthians 7:3-4 (Husband and wife give themselves to one another.)

Mosiah 18:21 (Hearts knit together in love.)

• What challenges arise when two people try to become one?
• Why did our family member and his/her fiancee decide to build a life together?
• How can the rest of us support them as they build their new life?

B. Supporting One Another

Ecclesiastes 4:9-12 (Two are better than one.)
Philippians. 2:1-4 (Look to the other's welfare.)
Mosiah 2:17-18 (Labor to serve one another.)

• In what ways do a married couple support one another?
• In what ways can a married couple serve one another?
• What goals do our family member and his/her fiancee have for their life together?

C. Putting on Charity
Matthew 7:24-27 or *3 Nephi 14:24-27* (Build your house upon the rock.)

Colossians 3:12-15 (Put on charity, the bond of perfectness.)

Moroni 7:45-48 (Moroni exhorts us to pray for charity.)

• What examples have we seen of couples treating each other with charity?

• How do couples in the world try to build marriages on foundations other than charity?

• Why do we need to pray for charity?

D. Inviting God into the Marriage
Matthew 18:19-20 (Where two gather in my name, I am in their midst.)

Revelation 3:20 (Jesus will sup with those who open their door to him.)

D&C 88:63 (Draw near unto me and I will draw near unto you.)

• What family traditions have invited the Savior into our home?

• What spiritual traditions will this new couple establish in their home?

• In what ways have the new couple sensed God's presence in their relationship?

E. The Covenant of Eternal Marriage
D&C 132:19-20 (The new and everlasting covenant of marriage.)

D&C 130:2 (That same sociality which exists here will exist there.)

D&C 90:24 (All things shall work for good if you remember the covenant.)

1 John 2:24-25 (God hath promised us eternal life.)

• What conditions and promises make up the covenant of eternal marriage?

• In what sense is a temple sealing a reaffirmation of the baptismal covenant?

• What qualities would we want to see in a marriage that will last forever?

• What difference will it make to know that our marriage has been sealed?

Discussions and Activities

A. Give a candle to your family member and another to his/her fiancee. Have them use these candles to together light a third candle. Explain that as the two flames came together to create a third flame, so your family member and his/her fiancee are about to create a new life together.

B. Have your family member and his/her fiancee write down promises or pledges that each makes to the other. Have other family members write down pledges of support for the couple in their new life together. Present these pledges to the new couple.

C. As a family, create a poster with the slogan, "Above all things, put on charity," or, "Cleave unto charity." Include drawings, photos, pictures from Church magazines, and so on, which represent the dimensions of charity listed in Moroni 7:45. Present the poster to the new couple. (Alternatively, family members could create a poster with the slogan, "Draw near unto me and I will draw near unto you.")

D. Present the new couple with a gift that will symbolize the Savior's presence in their home (for example, a painting, a set of scriptures, or a subscription to the *Ensign*).

E. On a piece of parchment, write out the conditions and promises of the covenant of eternal marriage, as if it were a contract signed by the Savior. Have your family member and his/her fiancee sign their names as well. Present the contract to them as a keepsake.

F. Give each member of the family the opportunity to welcome your family member's fiancee into the family and to wish the new couple well. Family members might consider doing this in the form of letters which the new couple could preserve as keepsakes.

G. Ask the new couple to explain why they decided to be married and what they hope to accomplish together. Family members who have already been married could be asked to speak on the same topic, as well as to describe how they continue to work to strengthen their marriages.

H. Encourage the new couple to reserve time during the wedding preparations and honeymoon to write in their journals. Encourage family members who are already married to use this occasion to record their latest reflections on their own marriages. Encourage other family members to reflect in their journals on their on-going preparation for temple marriage.

I. Read John 2:1-11, noting that Jesus performed his first miracle in order to contribute to the festivities surrounding a wedding. Discuss what contributions family members will make to the wedding and/or reception. During the closing prayer, ask that the Savior be present at the wedding festivities to share your family's joy.

J. Before offering the closing prayer, ask the new couple what prayers they feel in need of.

K. In lieu of a prayer, consider closing the devotional with a priesthood blessing for your family member.

Ideas for a Ring Ceremony

A ring ceremony can give friends and family the opportunity to express their joy and wishes on behalf of the new couple. It can also be a way to draw into the celebration guests who were unable to participate in the temple sealing.

Church policy establishes the following criteria for ring ceremonies (see *Ensign*, Oct. 1995, p. 24):

• A ring ceremony should be held at a location other than the temple. (An exception to this rule is a simple ring exchange done in the sealing room.)

• The circumstances of the ceremony should be consistent with the dignity of temple marriage.

• The ceremony should not appear to replicate any part of the marriage ceremony.

• The couple should not exchange vows during the ring ceremony.

Consider the following suggestions for making a ring ceremony a memorable spiritual experience.

A. Open with song and a prayer. In the prayer, thank God for having sealed the new couple in marriage.

B. Read any of the following passages of scripture:

• Isaiah 12:4-6 or 2 Nephi 22:4-6 (The Lord hath done excellent things.)

• Matthew 19:4-6 (What God hath joined together, let no one put asunder.)

• D&C 29:5-6 (Be glad, for I am in your midst.)

C. Invite a representative of the bride's family and a representative of the groom's family to congratulate the new couple on their marriage.

D. It would be appropriate for representatives of each family to say a few words about establishing a successful married life.

E. Immediately before the ring exchange, read any of the following:

- Ruth 1:16-17 (Whither thou goest, I will go.)
- Song of Solomon 8:6-7 (Many waters cannot quench love.)
- 1 John 4:7-8 (Every one that loveth knoweth God, for God is love.)
- Mosiah 18:21 (Hearts knit together in love.)
- D&C 88:125 (Clothe yourselves with the bond of charity.)

F. As the couple exchange rings, they could take the opportunity to express their love, thanks, or hopes. However, in keeping with Church guidelines, they should not exchange vows.

G. Allow time for family and friends to publicly voice their own congratulations, hopes, and wishes on behalf of the new couple.

H. Members of the bride's and groom's families could present gifts to the new couple symbolizing the beginning of their life together.

I. The new couple might take this opportunity to thank family and friends for sharing their joy and to announce any other festivities to follow.

J. Before closing, read any of the following:

- Numbers 6:24-26 (The Lord bless you and keep you.)
- 2 Corinthians 13:11 (The God of love and peace be with you.)
- Moroni 9:26 (May the grace of God abide with you.)
- D&C 61:36-37 (Be of good cheer; I am in your midst.)

K. Close with another song and prayer.

Creating a Family

Songs and Hymns
I Thank Thee, Dear Father (*Children's Songbook* 7)
Here We Are Together (*Children's Songbook* 261)

Because I Have Been Given Much (*Hymns* 219)
Love at Home (*Hymns* 294)
Families Can Be Together Forever (*Hymns* 300, *Children's Songbook* 188)
  I Am a Child of God (*Hymns* 301, *Children's Songbook* 2)
  I Know My Father Lives (*Hymns* 302, *Children's Songbook* 5)

Lesson Ideas
A. Creating a Child
Genesis 1:26-28 or *Moses 2:26-28* (Be fruitful and multiply.)
Psalms 127:3 (Children are a gift from the Lord.)
D&C 93:38-40 (Bring up your children in light and truth.)
• How do parents participate in the work of creation and of bringing to pass the eternal life of God's children?
• How will this new child be a gift and blessing to our family?
• How are we preparing ourselves for the responsibility of raising this child?

B. Adopting a Child
Exodus 2:1-10 (Moses was adopted by Pharaoh's daughter.)
Matthew 25:34-35 (I was a stranger, and ye took me in.)
1 Thessalonians 3:12 (The Lord make you to increase in love.)
• In what ways do we hope to bless the life of the child we are adopting?
• In what ways do we anticipate this child will be a blessing for our family?
• How can we extend our love to this new member of our family?

C. Sponsoring a Child
Matthew 25:37-40 (Inasmuch as ye have done it to one of the least of these.)
Luke 3:11 (He that hath two coats, impart to him that hath none.)
Mosiah 4:26 (I would that ye should impart of your substance.)
• Why does the Lord ask us to share our abundance with others?
• In what ways will our family's support bless the life of this child?
• How will supporting this child be a blessing for our family?

D. Opening Our Home to Someone In Need

Of the scriptures marked with an asterisk (*), choose the one that best applies to your situation: opening your home to a foster child, or to an aging family member.

Matthew 25:34-35 (I was a stranger, and ye took me in.)
*Mark 9:36-37 (Whosoever receiveth a child receiveth me.)
*John 19:25-27 (John took Mary into his home.)
Revelation 3:20 (I stand at the door and knock.)

- How will receiving this person into our home bless his/her life?
- How will this person's presence be a blessing for our family?
- In what sense are we opening our home to the Savior himself?

E. Creating a Blended Family

Colossians 3:12-15 (Put on charity, the bond of perfectness.)
Mosiah 2:17-18 (Labor to serve one another.)
D&C 38:25-27 (I say unto you, be one.)

- What conflicts and tensions are we likely to face as we bring our families together?
- In what ways can this union be a blessing for all of us?
- What do these scriptures teach us about how to become one?

F. Becoming an Eternal Family

Matthew 18:18 (Whatsoever ye bind on earth shall be bound in heaven.)
D&C 130:2 (The same sociality which exists here will exist there.)
D&C 132:19 (The new and everlasting covenant of marriage.)

- What promises do we receive—and make—when we are sealed in the temple?
- What qualities would we want to see in a family that will be together forever?
- What difference will it make to know that our family has been sealed?

Discussions and Activities

A. As part of the lesson, "Creating a Child," read Luke 1:39-44. Point out that a baby developing in the womb can hear—and respond to—what is happening outside the womb. Discuss the question: As this new child develops in its mother's womb, what can we do to provide a nurturing environment and to let it know it is loved?

B. As part of the lessons "Adopting a Child" or "Opening Our Home to Someone In Need," ask family members to remember a time when they spent the night in an unfamiliar place. What anxieties did they have? Discuss ways in which family members can help the newcomer feel less anxious or disoriented.

C. As part of the lesson, "Sponsoring a Child," prepare a framed photo of the child your family is sponsoring and arrange it near the family photo. Ask family members to do research on the child's home country and culture; have them share what they've learned during the devotional. Make a resolution to include the sponsored child in all family prayers.

D. As part of the lessons, "Creating a Child," "Adopting a Child," or "Opening Our Home to Someone In Need," discuss the changes, concerns, and new responsibilities which the newcomer's arrival may occasion.

E. As part of the lesson, "Creating a Blended Family," discuss the practical challenges of turning two families into a single household. What will it take from everyone to meet those challenges effectively?

F. In the case of a family preparing to go the temple, discuss such practical concerns as final preparations for the temple visit, the schedule of events, appropriate behavior in the temple, and so on. Children will have a more meaningful, less disorienting, temple experience if they have some tangible sense of what to expect—in other words, what they will see, hear, and do. A photograph of a sealing room, for instance, would be helpful, with a description of how family members will be arranged around the altar.

G. If you are using the lesson, "Creating a Child," give each family member the opportunity to express their hopes or wishes on behalf of the mother and developing child.

If you are using the lesson, "Adopting a Child" or "Opening Our Home to Someone In Need," give each family member an opportunity to formally welcome the newcomer.

If you are using the lesson, "Sponsoring a Child," give each family member an opportunity to express their hopes or wishes on behalf of the sponsored child.

H. Following the devotional (or the sealing), encourage family members to record in their journals their feelings about welcoming a new person into the family (or about becoming an eternal family).

I. If you are using the lesson, "Creating a Child," consider concluding with a priesthood blessing for the expectant mother, in lieu of a closing prayer.

Midlife

Songs and Hymns
I'm Thankful to Be Me (*Children's Songbook* 11)
I Will Follow God's Plan (*Children's Songbook* 164)
Now Thank We All Our God (*Hymns* 95)
More Holiness Give Me (*Hymns* 131)
Come, Let Us Anew (*Hymns* 217)
Have I Done Any Good? (*Hymns* 223)
Count Your Blessings (*Hymns* 241)

Lesson Ideas
A. Thanksgiving Despite Regrets
Matthew 7:9-11 or *3 Nephi 14:9-11* (Heavenly Father knows to give good gifts.)

2 Nephi 4:20-23, 26, 30 (Why should my heart weep?)

D&C 46:32 (Give thanks to God for whatsoever ye are blessed with.)

• In what ways have our family member's expectations of life fallen short of reality?

• What blessings have come to our family member, despite his/her disappointments?

• How has our family member been blessed in ways he/she never anticipated?

B. Letting Go and Moving On
Genesis 12:1, 4-5 or *Abraham 2:3-4, 15-16* (Abraham and Sarai took up their journey.)

1 Nephi 2:2-5 (Lehi and Sariah took up their journey.)

Philippians. 3:13-14 (Forgetting what is behind, reaching to what is before.)

- What dreams or aspirations has our family member had to give up over the years?
- In what sense is our family member, like Abraham and Sarai, or Lehi and Sariah, setting off in a new direction?
- How can we support our family member in his/her new spiritual journey?

C. Old Goals, New Goals

Psalms 37:3-5 (The Lord shall give thee the desires of thine heart.)

Moroni 7:33 (Ye shall have power to do whatsoever is expedient in me.)

D&C 11:8-10 (You shall be the means of doing much good.)

- How is a person in midlife particularly equipped to do good?
- What unrealized dreams would our family member still like to pursue in midlife?
- What new goals does our family member feel inspired to set for the coming years?

D. The Wisdom of Experience

Job 32:7 (Multitude of years should teach wisdom.)

Romans 8:28 (All things work together for good to them that love God.)

D&C 122:5-7 (All these things shall give thee experience.)

- How has our family member's life unfolded in ways he/she did not expect?
- What does our family member feel he/she has learned from these experiences?
- How do our family member's experiences equip him/her to serve others?

E. The Empty Nest

Psalms 127:3 (Children are an heritage of the Lord.)

Jeremiah 10:20 (My children are gone forth of me.)

Moses 5:11 (Despite hardship, Eve rejoiced that she could have seed.)

- How has our family member felt both taxed and enriched by parenting?

• With the children leaving home, what new plans does our family member have for personal development and service to others?

• How will our family maintain a sense of togetherness as we go our separate ways?

F. Facing Physical Change

Genesis 1:26-27 or *Moses 2:26-27* or *Abraham 4:26-27* (Created in God's image.)

1 Corinthians 3:16 (Know ye not that ye are the temple of God?)

D&C 93:11-14, 19-20 (We continue from grace to grace.)

• Why do many people feel negatively about the physical changes of midlife?

• What difference does it make to know that our bodies are in God's image?

• How does our society's obsession with staying young compare to what the restored gospel teaches us about eternal progression?

Discussions and Activities

A. Read D&C 11:8, 10. Point out that this passage refers to two kinds of gifts: gifts we have now and gifts we can have in the future. Invite your family member to make a list of gifts he/she would like to cultivate in the future. At the same time, have other family members make a list of gifts they see that their loved one has already been blessed with (talents, experiences, accomplishments, and so on).

B. As a family, create a time line of your family member's adulthood thus far, with the line running diagonally up the page (not horizontally across it). Label the time line, "I continue from grace to grace" (see D&C 93:13). Include on the time line accomplishments, disappointments, periods of adversity, signs of physical aging, and indications of spiritual maturity. Discuss the question: In what sense could it be said that every event on this time line represents a step forward in our loved one's eternal progress?

C. As a family, create a poster depicting a large tree, with the slogan "We do not cease to pray for you, that you might be fruitful in every good work" (see Colossians 1:9-10). Attach to the tree fruit-shaped cut-outs on which are written things that your family member would like to accomplish in the coming years.

D. As part of the lesson, "Letting Go and Moving On," invite your family member to compile two lists on separate sheets of paper. One list should be titled, "What I leave behind." The second should be titled, "What lies ahead."

While your family member compiles these lists, have the rest of the family create a poster depicting Abraham and Sarai, or Lehi and Sariah, traveling into the desert. Depict them moving from left to right, with ample space on both sides of the posterboard.

Finally, attach the two lists to the poster, "What I leave behind" on the left and "What lies ahead" on the right, with the traveling figures in the middle. Present the completed poster to your family member.

E. Ask your family member to prepare in advance a collage representing what he/she used to imagine his/her life would be like by now. During the devotional, have your family member interpret the collage.

Then create together a new collage to represent what your family member's life is actually like. If there are elements from the first collage that carry over to the second, cut those elements out of the first collage and physically transfer them to the second. Create new elements for the second collage as needed, to represent those aspects of his/her life your family member had not expected.

When the new collage is finished, compare it with the tattered remains of the old. How does your family member feel about those dreams he/she has never seen realized? How does he/she feel about the blessings that have come into his/her life instead?

F. Read Isaiah 53:3 (Mosiah 14:3) and Matthew 23:37. Discuss the question: As your family member mourns the loss of certain dreams and aspirations, what difference does it make to realize that Jesus also knew disappointment and grief?

G. Give everyone an opportunity to wish your family member well in this new phase of his/her life. Family members might consider doing this in the form of a letter.

H. In lieu of a prayer, consider closing with a priesthood blessing for your family member.

Retirement or Old Age

Songs and Hymns

Grandmother (*Children's Songbook* 200)
When Grandpa Comes (*Children's Songbook* 201)
Press Forward, Saints (*Hymns* 81)
Now Thank We All Our God (*Hymns* 95)
I Need Thee Every Hour (*Hymns* 98)
More Holiness Give Me (*Hymns* 131)
Come, Let Us Anew (*Hymns* 217)
Have I Done Any Good? (*Hymns* 223)

Lesson Ideas

A. Life After Retirement

Genesis 2:2 or *Moses 3:2* or *Abraham 5:2* (God rested from all his work.)

Alma 37:34 (Never be weary of good works.)

D&C 59:10 (Rest from your labors.)

• In what sense is retirement a kind of Sabbath?

• What does our family member look forward to doing after retirement?

• How will he/she continue to serve God and others in the coming years?

B. Continuing Growth

John 10:10 (I am come that they might have life more abundantly.)

2 Nephi 31:19-20 (Press forward with steadfastness in Christ.)

D&C 130:18-19 (Whatever intelligence we gain in life will rise with us.)

• How does the notion that the senior years are a time of decline compare with what the restored gospel teaches about eternal progression?

• What new goals would our family member like to pursue in the coming years?

• How can our family member continue to grow spiritually, mentally, and so on?

C. A Force for Good

Job 12:12 (In length of days is understanding.)
Matthew 10:39 (He that loseth his life for my sake shall find it.)
D&C 6:8-10 (You shall be the means of doing much good.)
• What knowledge and skills has our family member gained over the years?
• How does our family member's experience equip him/her to serve others?
• How does service make our lives more meaningful and satisfying?

D. Facing Physical Change

Genesis 1:26-27 or *Moses 2:26-27* or *Abraham 4:26-27* (Created in God's image.)
1 Corinthians 3:16 (Know ye not that ye are the temple of God?)
D&C 93:11-14, 19-20 (We continue from grace to grace.)
• Why do many people feel negatively about the physical changes of old age?
• What difference does it make to know that our bodies are in God's image?
• How does our society's obsession with staying young compare to what the restored gospel teaches us about eternal progression?

E. Thou Art My Trust

Psalms 71:5-9, 16-18 (Thou art my trust from my youth.)
Isaiah 46:4 (Even to your old age I will carry you.)
D&C 24:8 (I am with thee even unto the end of thy days.)
• What anxieties or concerns does our family member have about growing older?
• How has our family member drawn on God's strength and comfort in the past?
• How can our family member continue to cultivate a close relationship with God?

F. Caring for Our Loved One

Ruth 4:14-15 (Thy kinsman shall be a nourisher of thine old age.)
Galatians 6:2 (Bear ye one another's burdens.)

D&C 82:5 (Strengthen the feeble knees.)
- What special care does our family member require?
- Why is it important that we be involved in our family member's care?
- What resources are available to help us care for our family member?

G. Resisting Ageism

Jeremiah 31:13 (God will make young and old rejoice together.)
Alma 1:30 (The Lord's people were liberal to all, old and young.)
Moses 7:18 (The Lord's people were of one heart and one mind.)
- In what ways do people stereotype, demean, or patronize the elderly?
- In what sense are all people alike, regardless of age?
- How can our family foster a greater sense of oneness across generations?

Discussions and Activities

A. As a family, prepare a "retrospective" of your family member's life up to now. Areas to focus on might include:
- Childhood and adolescence.
- Educational achievements.
- Professional achievements.
- Raising a family.
- Church service.
- Talents and hobbies.
- Looking ahead to the future.

B. In preparation for the devotional, invite your family member to make a collage as follows: On the left half of the posterboard, place cut-outs, drawings, photos, and so on, which represent your family member's life up to now. On the right half of the posterboard, ask your family member to represent his/her goals or aspirations for the future. During the devotional, have your family member interpret the collage to the rest of the family.

C. Read Luke 2:25-38. Discuss the question: As a retiree or senior, what new opportunities will our family member have to bear witness of Christ and to do God's work, as Simeon and Ana did?

D. In the case of an older couple considering mission service, read the story of Aquila and Priscilla (Acts. 18; see also 1 Corinthians 16:19). Discuss the questions: What different kinds of service do missionary couples provide? What gifts, talents, or experience do this couple have which could be put to use in a mission?

E. Read Job 42:16. Invite your family member to comment on how he/she has felt watching the family grow through the years. This might be a good opportunity to discuss the question: How can we preserve or strengthen ties within our extended family, especially between grandparents and grandchildren?

F. Ask each person to write on a piece of paper something they would like to learn from, or do with, your aging family member. Present the slips of paper to your family member. Encourage him/her to make plans to teach or do these things.

G. Give each person an opportunity to wish your family member happiness, success, and fulfilment for the coming years.

H. Encourage family members still in the workforce to reflect in their journals on their own preparations for retirement. Encourage younger family members (adolescents or college students) to reflect in their journals on the kinds of memories they would like to have to look back on when they reach retiring age.

I. In the spirit of D&C 101:72 ("Let these things be done in their time, but not in haste; and observe to have all things prepared before you"), this might be a good occasion for retirees or seniors to meet with their children to discuss such matters as wills, advance directives, preferred options for assisted care, and funeral and burial arrangements.

J. As part of the lesson, "Caring for Our Loved One," read John 21:18. Discuss the question: As our family member comes to depend more and more on the assistance of others, how can we help him/her retain a sense of dignity?

K. In lieu of a prayer, consider closing with a priesthood blessing for your aging family member.

Preparing for Death

Songs and Hymns

I Lived in Heaven (*Children's Songbook* 4)
Did Jesus Really Live Again? (*Children's Songbook* 64)
I Need Thee Every Hour (*Hymns* 98)
Nearer, My God, to Thee (*Hymns* 100)
The Lord Is My Shepherd (*Hymns* 108)
Be Still, My Soul (*Hymns* 124)
I Know That My Redeemer Lives (*Hymns* 136)
Abide with Me! (*Hymns* 166)
As the Shadows Fall (*Hymns* 168)
O My Father (*Hymns* 292)

Lesson Ideas

A. A Time to Die

Genesis 3:19 or *Moses 4:25* (Unto dust shalt thou return.)
Ecclesiastes 3:1-2 (A time to be born, a time to die.)
Matthew 7:9-11 or *3 Nephi 14:9-11* (Heavenly Father knows to give good gifts.)
• If death is a natural part of life, why are people often reluctant to discuss it?
• What would it mean to prepare for death the way we prepare for other major life transitions like adulthood, marriage, and retirement?
• How can we bring ourselves to accept death when it comes in an unexpected time or way?

B. Looking Back on a Life

Revelation 20:12 (Each of our lives is recorded.)
1 Nephi 1:1 (Nephi was both afflicted and blessed in his days.)
D&C 58:3 (Ye cannot behold for the present the design of God.)
• What is the story of our family member's life?
• What adversity and blessings has our family member experienced?

• How can we find peace when life takes unwanted or seemingly senseless turns?

C. Unfinished Business

Job 16:22 (I go the way whence I shall not return.)
Hebrews 4:15-16 (Let us come boldly to the throne of grace.)
Alma 12:24 (A time to prepare to meet God.)
• What would our family member still like to see or do before he/she dies?
• Are there things he/she would like to try to make right before passing on?
• How can trust in God's grace help our family member come to terms with regrets?

D. Saying Goodbye

D&C 107:53-56 (Adam met with his posterity before dying.)
1 Kings 2:1-3 (David left a final charge with Solomon.)
2 Nephi 4:12 (Lehi spoke to all his family before dying.)
Jacob 7:27 (Jacob passed the plates on to Enos before dying.)
Moroni 10:34 (Moroni bade readers farewell.)
• What final words would our family member like to leave with family and friends?
• What personal possessions would our family member like to pass on to others?
• How would each of us like to say goodbye to our family member?

E. Watch with Me

Ecclesiastes 7:4 (The heart of the wise is in the house of mourning.)
Matthew 26:36-38 (Tarry ye here, and watch with me.)
Mosiah 18:8-10 (Are ye willing to mourn with those that mourn?)
• Why are people inclined to distance themselves from someone who is dying?
• How can we show our family member that we support him/her during this time?
• What is the difference between enjoying our final days with our family member and pretending that nothing is wrong?

F. Thou Art with Me

Psalms 23 (Though I walk through the valley of the shadow of death.)

Romans 14:8-9 (Whether we live or die, we are the Lord's.)

2 Nephi 1:14-15 (I am encircled about eternally in the arms of his love.)

• What does it mean to say that we are the Lord's?

• What difference does it make to know that God is with our family member?

• How can trust in God help our family member face death?

G. Going Home to God

Ecclesiastes 12:7 (The spirit shall return unto God.)

John 14:1-2 (In my Father's house I prepare a place for you.)

Alma 40:11 (The spirits of all are taken home to God.)

• What difference does it make to think of death as a homecoming?

• Why is death nevertheless an occasion for sorrow?

• What experiences, traits, talents, or memories will our family member take with him/her when he/she goes back to God?

H. I Go to My Rest

Revelation 14:13 (They may rest from their labours.)

Enos 1:27 (I soon go to the place of my rest.)

D&C 124:86 (They shall rest from all their labors here.)

• In what sense will death bring rest to our family member?

• Why is death nevertheless an occasion for regret and grief?

• What comfort does D&C 124:86 offer someone who feels he/she is leaving things undone?

I. Death, Where Is Thy Sting?

Isaiah 25:8 (God will wipe away tears from off all faces.)

1 Corinthians 15:55-58 (Death, where is thy sting?)

Mosiah 16:7-8 (The sting of death is swallowed up in Christ.)

• What does it mean to say that the sting of death is "swallowed up" in Christ?

• How does our faith in Christ help us face death?

• Why is death an occasion for sorrow, notwithstanding our faith?

J. Dying with Christ

2 Timothy 2:11 (If we be dead with him, we shall also live with him.)

Alma 7:11-12 (He will take upon him death.)

D&C 18:11 (The Lord your Redeemer suffered death.)

• What difference does it make to know that the Savior also experienced death?

• In what sense does the experience of death make us one with Christ?

• What does Paul mean when he says that if we die with Christ, we will also live with him?

Discussions and Activities

A. Read or recount the story of Jesus walking with the disciples on the road to Emmaus (Luke 24:13-35). Discuss the following questions:

• In what sense is our family member, like the disciples, in the midst of a difficult journey?

• What would it mean for us to accompany our family member on this journey, the way Jesus accompanied the disciples?

• What would it mean for us to abide with our family member?

• In what sense is the Lord made known to us as we share this experience together?

B. Read Matthew 26:36-39. Discuss the following questions: What regrets or fears does our family member have about dying? What difference does it make to know that Jesus, too, experienced sorrow and fear as he approached death?

C. Invite your loved one to share aloud his/her fears about dying. Then invite other family members to share aloud their fears about your loved one's death. After everyone has expressed their feelings, read D&C 101:36. Discuss the question: What comfort does this passage offer us?

D. Read Job 10:20-21. Discuss the question: How can we balance our need to spend time with our family member with the need our family member may have for privacy, solitude, quiet, rest?

E. Read or retell Matthew 25:31-40. Ask family members to recount ways in which they have seen the one who is dying serve others during his/her life.

F. Read D&C 138:11-16 and discuss the question: Whom do we picture waiting to greet our family member into the spirit world (ancestors, friends, and so on)? Prepare a drawing of this reunion to present to your family member.

G. Read Luke 23:46 and discuss the questions: What would it mean for our family member to commend his/her spirit to God? What would it mean for the rest of us to commend our family member's spirit to God?

H. If your loved one's age and health permit, encourage him/her to keep a journal. The final thoughts and experiences your loved one records will be especially meaningful to other family members once he/she has passed on. Likewise, encourage other family members to write periodically in their journals about the experience of being with their loved one as he/she approaches death.

I. Discuss with your family member his/her wishes with regards to funeral arrangements. Genesis 49:28-33 might provide a scriptural basis for this discussion.

J. Being "free to choose" (2 Nephi 2:27) includes being able to exercise a certain degree of control over the circumstances of our death. Explore the options available for helping your family member have the kind of death he/she wants: home care, palliative care, advance directives, and so on.

K. The scriptures enjoin us to "seek learning, even by study" (D&C 88:118) and assure us that "if [we] are prepared [we] shall not fear" (D&C 38:30). In the spirit of these passages, approach your family member's physician, visit your local library, or search on-line for information about what your family member is likely to experience in the process of dying. How can your family member, and those who surround him/her, cope with the physical changes that lead to the moment of death?

L. In lieu of a prayer, consider closing the devotional with a priesthood blessing for your dying family member—not a health blessing, necessarily, but a blessing of comfort and guidance.

Times of Adversity

Loss of a Dream

Songs and Hymns

I Will Follow God's Plan (*Children's Songbook* 164)
Lead, Kindly Light (*Hymns* 97)
Nearer, My God, to Thee (*Hymns* 100)
Cast Thy Burden upon the Lord (*Hymns* 110)
Come, Ye Disconsolate (*Hymns* 115)
Be Still, My Soul (*Hymns* 124)
Where Can I Turn for Peace? (*Hymns* 129)
Be Thou Humble (*Hymns* 130)
I Know My Father Lives (*Hymns* 302, *Children's Songbook* 5)

Lesson Ideas

A. Working through Grief

Genesis 35:3 (In the day of my distress, God went with me.)
2 Nephi 4:20 (God hath led me through mine afflictions.)
D&C 88:4-6 (Christ is in all and through all.)

• What does it mean to "work through" grief?

• In what sense is our loved one traveling through a wilderness (2 Nephi 4:20)?

• What difference does it make to know that the Savior and our Heavenly Father are with our loved one?

B. Sharing Our Loved One's Grief

Genesis 37:34-35 (Jacob's children tried unsuccessfully to comfort him.)
Romans 12:15 (Weep with them that weep.)
Mosiah 18:8-10 (Mourn with those that mourn.)

• What clichés might people be inclined to offer our loved one during this time?

- Why are those clichés not really helpful?
- How can we show our loved one that we share his/her grief?

C. God Grieves This Loss

Isaiah 53:3-4 or *Mosiah 14:3-4* (Surely he has borne our griefs.)
D&C 133:52-53 (In all their afflictions he was afflicted.)
Moses 7:28-31 (Enoch saw that God wept.)

- The Lord has an eternal perspective—yet he shares our loved one's grief. Why?
- What difference does it make to know that God feels our disappointments?
- In what sense is God "carrying" our loved one (D&C 133:53)?

D. Healing the Broken Heart

Proverbs 13:12 (Hope deferred maketh the heart sick.)
Luke 4:16-21 (Jesus came to heal the broken-hearted.)
Alma 17:10 (The Lord said, Be comforted.)

- What does it mean to "heal" following the loss of a dream?
- How can our loved one's relationship with the Savior provide comfort?
- How can it help our loved one find the strength to cope?

E. Letting Go and Moving On

Genesis 12:1, 4-5 or *Abraham 2:3-4, 15-16* (Abraham and Sarai took up their journey.)
1 Nephi 2:2-5 (Lehi and Sariah took up their journey.)
Philippians 3:13-14 (Forgetting what is behind, reaching to what is before.)

- What dreams must Abraham and Sarai, or Lehi and Sariah, have given up when they started their new journey?
- In what sense is our loved one setting off on a new journey?
- How can we support our loved one as he/she presses forward with his/her life?

F. Seeking Direction

Isaiah 42:16 (I will lead them in ways they have not known.)
Isaiah 48:17 or *1 Nephi 20:17* (God leadeth thee by the way thou shouldst go.)
D&C 78:17-18 (I will lead you along.)

- How does our loved one's loss require him/her to seek new direction in life?
- How can we support or assist our loved one as he/she searches for direction?
- What difference does it make to know that, whether or not we can see it, God is leading our loved one along?

G. Trusting God's Providence

Matthew 7:9-11 or *3 Nephi 14:9-11* (Heavenly Father knows to give good gifts.)

Romans 8:26, 28 (All things work for good to them that love God.)

D&C 58:3 (Ye cannot behold for the present the design of your God.)

- What difference does it make to know that God has a plan for our loved one?
- Why does that knowledge not simply "erase" our loved one's disappointment?
- What would a life based on trust in God's providence look like?

Discussions and Activities

A. Read Isaiah 53:3 (Mosiah 14:3) and Matthew 23:37. Discuss the question: As our loved one mourns the loss of his/her dream, what difference does it make to realize that Jesus also knew disappointment and grief?

B. Explain to your family that different people experience grief in different ways, but that grief generally unfolds in three stages:

　　1. In the face of a loss, a person's first reaction will generally be shock. This might take the form of numbness or denial.
　　2. Once the reality of the loss has set in, the person may experience a variety of emotions: anger, fear, guilt, depression, exhaustion, or despair. The person may have the sense that his/her life has fallen apart.
　　3. Little by little, the person will reconstruct his/her life. The heartache will lessen as the person comes to accept the loss. The person will recover his/her ability to live with joy.

Emphasize that this process takes time and energy, and that it is unrealistic to expect a person to quickly "get over" the loss of a cherished dream. Discuss the questions: How can we support our loved one as he/she works through this process? In what sense could it be said that working through grief is a kind of rebirth?

C. Read or retell Ezekiel's vision of the dry bones brought back to life (Ezekiel 37:1-14). Explain that Ezekiel's vision, like Lehi's dream, uses symbols to convey gospel truths. Discuss the following questions:

• What do the dry bones in the vision represent (v. 11)?

• How could we liken the vision to what our loved one is experiencing?

• In what sense could it be said that our loved one is undergoing a kind of resurrection?

D. Ask your loved one to compile a list of words or phrases to describe the identity that he/she thought he/she was going to have, or that he/she wanted to have. At the same time, invite other family members to compile lists of words or phrases to describe their own sense of who your loved one is.

Compare the list your loved one compiled with the lists compiled by other family members. Then read Isaiah 64:8. Discuss the following questions:

• What do we learn from other family members' lists about the gifts, traits, or talents God has given our loved one?

• Which of the words or phrases on our loved one's list still describe him/her?

• How can our loved one seek God's guidance in discovering and developing the identity meant for him/her?

E. Invite each family member to write a letter to your loved one. In these letters, family members could express their feelings about the loved one's loss and pledge their support as the loved one seeks new direction in life.

F. Discuss the questions: If our loved one were mourning a death, what steps might he/she take to preserve the memory of the one who died? What can our loved one do to preserve the memory of the lost dream?

G. As part of the lesson, "Healing the Broken Heart," invite your loved one to create a drawing to represent his/her feelings about the loss. Other family members might do the same to represent their feelings about what your loved one is going through. Title each drawing, "Hope deferred maketh the heart sick" (Proverbs 13:12).

Have family members hang their drawings near their beds, where they will see them during personal prayers. Encourage family members to pray regularly on behalf of your loved one.

H. As part of the lesson, "Trusting God's Providence," read Matthew 26:39. Discuss the question: When our lives do not unfold in the way we had hoped or anticipated, how can we come to accept this? What difference does it make to know that even Jesus found it difficult to accept God's plan for his life?

I. In lieu of a prayer, consider closing with a priesthood blessing for your loved one.

Miscarriage or Stillbirth

Songs and Hymns
God Is Watching Over All (*Children's Songbook* 229)
Nearer, My God, to Thee (*Hymns* 100)
The Lord Is My Shepherd (*Hymns* 108)
Cast Thy Burden upon the Lord (*Hymns* 110)
Come, Ye Disconsolate (*Hymns* 115)
Be Still, My Soul (*Hymns* 124)
Where Can I Turn for Peace? (*Hymns* 129)
Families Can Be Together Forever (*Hymns* 300, *Children's Songbook* 188)

Lesson Ideas
A. Mourning Our Loss
Jeremiah 31:15 or *Matthew 2:18* (Rachel weeping for her children.)

Romans 12:15 (Weep with them that weep.)

Mosiah 18:8-10 (Mourn with those that mourn.)

• Why is it important that we allow ourselves to mourn this loss, however insignificant it may seem to others?

• How can we support one other during this time?

• What does it mean to share someone else's sorrow?

B. God Grieves with Us

Isaiah 53:3-4 or *Mosiah 14:3-4* (Surely he has borne our griefs.)
D&C 133:52-53 (In all their afflictions he was afflicted.)
Moses 7:28-31 (Enoch saw that God wept.)

• The Lord has an eternal perspective on life and death—yet he grieves with us. Why?

• What difference does it make to know that God mourns our loss with us?

• What difference does it make to realize that the Father, too, lost his Child?

C. Working through Grief

Genesis 35:3 (In the day of my distress, God went with me.)
D&C 24:8 (Be patient in afflictions, for I am with thee.)
D&C 88:4-6 (Christ is in all and through all.)

• What does it mean to "work through" grief?

• How long can we expect this process to take?

• What difference does it make to know that the Savior and our Heavenly Father are with us no matter how difficult things get?

D. Healing the Aching Heart

Psalms 147:3 (He healeth the broken in heart.)
Malachi 4:2 or *3 Nephi 25:2* (The Son shall arise with healing in his wings.)
1 Nephi 8:24 (They did press forward through the darkness.)

• Why does it not necessarily hurt less to have lost our child before he/she was born?

• Why is it unrealistic to expect that we will simply "get over" this loss?

• How can we draw on the Savior's healing power as we press forward with our lives?

E. Comfort Will Come

Matthew 5:4 or *3 Nephi 12:4* (Blessed are they that mourn.)
Matthew 11:28 (Come unto me; I will give you rest.)
John 14:18 (I will not leave you comfortless.)

• How long can we expect it will take for our grief to give way to comfort?

• How can we stay close to the Savior as we work through our grief?

• What difference do gospel teachings make as we cope with this loss?

Discussions and Activities

A. Decide what kind of funeral rites you would like to observe following the loss of your child. In the case of a miscarriage, a family may not have the option of burying their child. Still, you may find it comforting to hold a memorial service of some kind, be it in a hospital chapel, at home, or in a favorite spot outdoors.

B. Explain to your family that different people experience grief in different ways, but that grief generally unfolds in three stages:

    1. Family members may initially feel shock. This could take the form of numbness or denial.

    2. Once the reality of the loss has set in, family members will begin to feel the pain of the loss. They may experience anger, fear, guilt, depression, exhaustion, or despair. These feelings may recur over months or even years.

    3. Little by little, family members will reconstruct their lives. Their heartache will lessen as they come to accept the loss. They will recover their ability to live with joy.

Emphasize that some family members will feel the loss of the pregnancy more strongly than others and will, therefore, grieve longer. Discuss the questions: How can family members help each other as we work through this process? In what sense could it be said that working through grief is a kind of resurrection?

C. Take steps to preserve your child's memory. These might include giving your child a name; preserving footprints or photos in family albums; keeping physical objects, such as blankets, that remind you of the pregnancy; or purchasing a doll or ornament to memorialize the child.

D. Express your feelings in the form of a letter, or a series of letters, to your child.

E. Read Psalms 22:10. Discuss the questions: What difference does it make to know that God was our child's God even before he/she was born? What difference does it make to know that God is still our child's God?

F. Read Psalms 40:1-2 and Psalms 94:17-19. Record in your journal whatever thoughts and feelings come to you from reading these passages. You might find it helpful to repeat this activity at intervals as you work through your grief.

G. A woman who has lost a pregnancy may worry that she is somehow responsible for what has happened. Read 3 Nephi 17:5-7 and discuss the question: How can the Savior bring healing to someone afflicted with self-recrimination?

H. In the case of a miscarriage, read Matthew 10:29 or Luke 12:6. Discuss the question: When others may treat our loss as insignificant, what difference does it make to know that the loss of even a sparrow matters to God?

I. It has been estimated that as many as one out of every four pregnancies ends in miscarriage. In what sense is this helpful to know? In what sense is it not helpful?

J. In the case of a stillbirth, consider the following statement by President Joseph Fielding Smith:

There is no information given by revelation in regard to the status of stillborn children. However, I will express my personal opinion that we should have hope that *these little ones will receive a resurrection and then belong to us.* I cannot help feeling that this will be the case. (Doctrines of Salvation, vol. 2, p. 280; emphasis in original)

K. Following the loss of a pregnancy, anniversaries such as the anticipated delivery date, or the date on which the pregnancy was lost, may become painful. On such occasions, consider the following ideas for memorializing your loss:

• Read Malachi 4:5-6 or 3 Nephi 25:5-6. Discuss the question: What can I do today to "turn my heart" to the child I lost? Why do I feel it is important to preserve my child's memory?

• Observe a minute of silence in your child's memory, perhaps after lighting a candle.

• Draw a picture of your child as you imagine he/she might have grown up to become. Alternatively, you could draw a picture of what you imagine your child's spirit is doing now.

• Write a letter to your child, expressing to him/her your feelings about the pregnancy and the loss.

• Make a donation of time or money to an organization that works to improve prenatal care, or that provides support to people who have lost a pregnancy.

• Offer a prayer thanking God for the joy your pregnancy brought you. Pray for help in coping with the loss. Pray on behalf of the child you lost. Pray that your child will feel your love reaching out to him/her across the veil.

L. If there are other children in the family, keep in mind that they, too, have suffered a loss—the loss of a brother or sister whose arrival they looked forward to. Invite them to participate in the process of mourning and memorializing your child.

When a Pregnancy Must Be Terminated

Church policy recognizes that under certain circumstances, a pregnancy may need to be terminated. Those circumstances are rape, incest, situations where the mother's life is in jeopardy, or cases where a fetus is not viable. The decision to terminate a pregnancy is, of course, an extremely difficult one. Couples or individuals facing this decision are directed to counsel with their ecclesiastical leaders and to seek the guidance of the Spirit (see "Abortion," Encyclopedia of Mormonism, vol. 1, p. 7; also, Boyd K. Packer, *Ensign*, Nov. 1990, p. 85).

When a pregnancy must be terminated, it is natural for family members to experience grief, anxiety, or regret; this is especially true of the expectant mother. Expectant parents who have concluded that they need to terminate a pregnancy may find it helpful to consider the following:

A. The lesson ideas and ideas for reflection which appear above may be applicable, especially in the case of a pregnancy that is being terminated because the mother's life is in danger or because the fetus is not viable. Many of the devotional ideas which appear in the section of this book titled "Victimization" will be applicable to cases of rape or sexual abuse.

B. Latter-day Saints may be troubled about the consequences that terminating the pregnancy will have for the spirit that would have inhabited this body. Spencer W. Kimball declared that "insofar as eternity is concerned, no soul will be deprived of rich and high and eternal blessings for anything which that person could not help" (*Ensign*, Oct. 1979, p. 5). Discuss the question: In light of the unknowns we face regarding the eternal status of this unborn child, what comfort does President Kimball's statement provide?

C. Read Luke 23:46. Discuss the questions: In what sense are we commending this unborn child into our Heavenly Father's hands? How can we say good-bye to the possibilities this pregnancy represented for us? How can we seek God's support as we mourn this loss?

D. The expectant mother may find it helpful to read Alma 7:11-12 and to reflect on the question: What difference does it make to realize that the Savior shares with me the pain—both physical and emotional—of this experience?

E. The expectant mother may want to receive a health blessing before the pregnancy is terminated, to comfort her as she undergoes the procedure and to aid her recovery. (See "Ideas for a Health Blessing," in the section of this book titled "Illness or Disability.")

Death of a Family Member

Songs and Hymns
Did Jesus Really Live Again? (*Children's Songbook* 64)
Nearer, My God, to Thee (*Hymns* 100)
The Lord Is My Shepherd (*Hymns* 108)
Cast Thy Burden upon the Lord (*Hymns* 110)
Come, Ye Disconsolate (*Hymns* 115)
Be Still, My Soul (*Hymns* 124)
Where Can I Turn for Peace? (*Hymns* 129)
I Know That My Redeemer Lives (*Hymns* 136)
Each Life That Touches Ours for Good (*Hymns* 293)
Families Can Be Together Forever (*Hymns* 300, *Children's Songbook* 188)

Lesson Ideas
A. A Time to Mourn
2 Samuel 18:33 (David mourned for Absalom.)
Jeremiah 31:15 or *Matthew 2:18* (Rachel weeping for her children.)
John 11:33-36 (Jesus wept at Lazarus' tomb.)
D&C 42:45 (Weep for the loss of them that die.)

• What different emotions can people experience as the result of a loved one's death?

• Why is it important that we allow ourselves to express these emotions?

• How can we express these emotions in healthy ways?

B. Mourning Together

Genesis 37:34-35 (Jacob's children tried unsuccessfully to comfort him.)

Romans 12:15 (Weep with them that weep.)

Mosiah 18:8-10 (Mourn with those that mourn.)

• Why are clichés not really helpful to someone who is grieving?

• How can showing that you share someone's sorrow be a comfort to them?

• How can we mourn the loss of our loved one with one another?

C. God Grieves with Us

Isaiah 53:3-4 or *Mosiah 14:3-4* (Surely he has borne our griefs.)

D&C 133:52-53 (In all their afflictions he was afflicted.)

Moses 7:28-31 (Enoch saw that God wept.)

• The Lord has an eternal perspective on life and death—yet he grieves with us. Why?

• What difference does it make to know that God mourns with our family?

• How does the experience of mourning make us one with God and Christ?

D. Working through Grief

Genesis 35:3 (In the day of my distress, God went with me.)

D&C 24:8 (Be patient in afflictions, for I am with thee.)

D&C 88:4-6 (Christ is in all and through all.)

• What does it mean to "work through" the grief caused by a loved one's death?

• How long can we expect this process to take?

• What difference does it make to know that the Savior and our Heavenly Father are with us, no matter how difficult things get?

E. Adapting and Healing

Psalms 147:3 (He healeth the broken in heart.)

Malachi 4:2 or *3 Nephi 25:2* (The Son shall arise with healing in his wings.)

1 Nephi 8:24 (They did press forward through the darkness.)

• What changes do we need to make as a result of our loved one's death?

• Will we ever "get over" our loved one's absence?

• How can we draw on the Savior's healing power as we press forward with our lives?

F. Comfort Will Come

Matthew 5:4 or *3 Nephi 12:4* (Blessed are they that mourn.)

Matthew 11:28 (Come unto me; I will give you rest.)

John 14:18 (I will not leave you comfortless.)

• How long can we expect it will take for our grief to give way to comfort?

• How can we stay close to the Savior as we work through our grief?

• What difference do gospel teachings make as we cope with our loved one's death?

G. Our Loved One Is with God

Genesis 25:8-10 (Abraham died and was gathered to his people.)

1 Thessalonians 5:9-11 (Whether we wake or sleep, we live with him.)

Alma 40:11 (Taken home to that God who gave them life.)

• What difference does it make to know that our loved one is with God and other family members?

• Why do we mourn our loved one's death in spite of that knowledge?

• Why does Paul say that the living and the dead live together with God?

H. A Future Reunion

1 Thessalonians 4:13-14 (Those who sleep in Jesus will God bring with him.)

Moroni 10:34 (I bid you farewell until I meet you before the pleasing bar.)

D&C 130:2 (That same sociality which exists here will exist there.)

• What difference does it make to know that we will be with our loved one again?

• Why do we mourn our loved one's death in spite of that knowledge?

• How can we use our loved one's funeral as a chance to bid him/her farewell?

Discussions and Activities

A. Discuss what involvement family members will have in the funeral services. To make the experience less distressing for children, give them a concrete sense of what to expect: what they will see, what they will hear, where they will be, who will be with them, and so on.

B. Invite each family member to write a farewell letter to the one who has died. These letters might be placed in your loved one's casket, or family members might prefer to keep the letters in their own journals.

C. Read the following scriptural examples of different ways in which people might be affected by grief:
• Genesis 49:33-50:1 (Needing to touch the body.)
• 2 Samuel 18:33 (Wishing you had died instead.)
• Job 6:2-3 (Feeling overwhelmed, speechless.)
• Job 6:11 (Feeling hopeless, without purpose.)
• Job 7:4 (Unable to sleep.)
• Job 7:11 (Needing to talk.)
• Job 7:13-14 (Nightmares.)
• Job 9:16-17 (A loss of faith.)
• Job 13:4 (Denial, anger at others.)
• Job 19:6-10 (Feeling angry with God.)
• Job 23:8-9 (Feeling abandoned by God.)
• Job 30:15-16 (Fear for the future.)
• Psalms 6:2-3, 6 (Depression, physical exhaustion.)
• John 11:21 (Replaying in your mind what might have been.)

Emphasize that these are normal reactions to a loved one's death and that in time they will pass. Discuss ways in which family members can demonstrate patience and support for one another as they each react to their loved one's death.

D. In our society, men and boys often feel that they have to "be strong"—in other words, to remain composed in the face of a loved one's death. Use the following scriptural examples to assure male members of your family that there is no reason they cannot cry or otherwise express grief:
  • Genesis 50:1 (Joseph became distraught at Jacob's death.)
  • 2 Samuel 18:33 (David cried out loud for Absalom's death.)
  • Psalms 88:1-3 (The Psalmist cried day and night.)
  • John 11:33-36 (Jesus wept at Lazarus' tomb.)
  • Moses 7:28 (The God of heaven wept.)

E. Explain to your family that different people experience grief in different ways, but that grief generally unfolds in three stages:
  1. Family members may initially feel shock. This could take the form of numbness or denial.
  2. Once the reality of the death has set in, family members will begin to feel the pain of the loss. They may experience anger, fear, guilt, depression, exhaustion, or despair. These feelings may recur over months or even years.
  3. Little by little, family members will reconstruct their lives. Their heartache will lessen as they come to accept the loss. They will recover their ability to live with joy.

Emphasize that this process takes time and energy, and that it is unrealistic to expect that family members will quickly "get over" their loved one's death. Discuss the questions: How can we support each other as we work through this process? In what sense could it be said that working through grief is a kind of resurrection?

F. Read Genesis 49:33-50:14. Note that ancient mourning customs were based on the understanding that mourning is a lengthy process. By contrast, our fast-paced modern society expects people to move on with their lives quickly after a loved one's death. Discuss the question: How can we make time to mourn and still keep up with our day-to-day responsibilities?

G. Explain that while family members naturally want to support each other in their grief, their ability to do so will be limited by the fact that they are all feeling debilitated. Discuss where, outside the home, family members might turn for additional support.

H. Encourage family members to write frequently in their journals during the coming months, as a way of expressing their changing feelings about their loved one's death.

I. Read Romans 15:4 and D&C 136:29. Encourage family members to pay special attention to personal prayer and scripture study as they cope with their grief.

J. Emphasize how important it is that family members take good care of themselves physically during their time of grief. Invite family members to set (or renew) goals related to physical fitness and nutrition. 2 Samuel 12:15-23 could serve as the scriptural basis for this discussion.

K. As it seems appropriate, discuss the practical matters that need to be addressed in the wake of your loved one's death (disposing of your loved one's possessions; contacting employers, teachers, and others; rearranging family responsibilities; handling financial matters). Mosiah 4:27 could set the tone for this discussion.

L. Read Job 7:11. Assure your family that they are free to talk about their loved one's death, their feelings about the death, or their memories of the loved one. Explain that talking about these things is an important part of healing. (On the other hand, don't press family members to talk about the death before they feel ready to do so.) In particular, do not be afraid to use the word "dead." Using euphemisms reinforces the notion that death is somehow taboo or unspeakable.

M. Consider the following suggestions for discussing a loved one's death with young children:

• Avoid euphemisms that could confuse children about what has happened—euphemisms such as, "Daddy's left us," "Mommy's gone to sleep," or "Grandma's gone to heaven."

• Explain that when a person's spirit leaves their body, the body stops working and gradually rots away. This is why we bury (or cremate) the bodies of people who have died.

• Take care that in teaching about the resurrection, you do not give children the impression that their loved one is going to return at any moment. Be clear in explaining that you will not see your loved one again in this lifetime.

- Assure children that they did not cause the loved one's death, and that the loved one did not leave because he/she did not love the family.
- Avoid saying that God "took" the loved one. This can lead children to fear or resent God. Speak instead of the loved one having gone back home to God.
- A loved one's death may cause children to fear that they, or someone else in the family, will die soon. Assure children that it will likely be a long time before anyone else in the family dies.
- Children may worry about what will become of them should both their parents die. Discuss how your child would be cared for should that ever happen.
- Don't be afraid to admit that we have many unanswered questions about death. Express your testimony that Heavenly Father loves his children and has a plan for our happiness, even though we don't always understand why things happen the way they do.

N. In the spirit of the injunction to "seek learning, even by study" (D&C 88:118), visit your local library, or search on-line, for information about coping with the death of a loved one.

Ideas for a Memorial

Holidays, birthdays, and anniversaries may become difficult after a loved one's death, because they highlight the loved one's absence. One way to cope with this is to incorporate a memorial of your loved one into the holiday celebration. A memorial could also be held on the anniversary of your loved one's death, as a way for family members to grieve together, comfort one another, and experience the blessing of the loved one's memory.

A memorial might be a simple gesture taking only a few moments, or it might be a whole family home evening. Consider the following list of ideas.

A. Incorporate some of your loved one's favorite food items into your meals that day.

B. Visit, or gather in, a place your loved one was fond of.

C. Sing a song or hymn your loved one was fond of.

D. Read Malachi 4:5-6 (3 Nephi 25:5-6). Discuss the question: What can we do in the course of this day to "turn our hearts" to our loved one?

E. Observe a minute of silence in your loved one's memory, perhaps after lighting a candle.

F. Invite family members to recount, or draw, fond memories of their loved one. This might be an opportune moment to discuss how family members are coping with the death.

G. Read D&C 138:57. Invite family members to describe personality traits, talents, or spiritual gifts your loved one possessed which would equip him/her to do the Lord's work in the spirit world.

H. Write a letter to your loved one, "updating" him/her on what's been happening in your life.

I. Compose a simple poem in memory of your loved one by making a list of specific things your remember about him/her. Head each item in the list, "I remember" (or, depending on how you are feeling at the time, "I miss"). For example:

I remember the house full of the new furniture he'd built, waiting to be delivered.

I remember how much he loved to sing "Secret Prayer."

I remember his dazed grin after he was married.

I remember his crazy plan to open an ice cream parlor.

I remember how quick he was to laugh, even when things were going badly.

J. Make a donation of time or money to a charity you associate with your loved one.

K. During family prayer, thank God for the blessings and joy that your loved one brought into your lives. Express the anticipation with which you look forward to being with your loved one again someday. Pray that your loved one will feel your love reaching out to him/her across the veil. You might even pray that your loved one will be happy and successful in whatever work he/she is doing beyond the veil.

Death of a Pet

Songs and Hymns
My Heavenly Father Loves Me (*Children's Songbook* 228)
God Is Watching Over All (*Children's Songbook* 229)

All Things Bright and Beautiful (*Children's Songbook* 231)
All Creatures of Our God and King (*Hymns* 62)
God Is Love (*Hymns* 87)
Each Life That Touches Ours for Good (*Hymns* 293)

Lesson Ideas

A. Bidding Farewell to a Friend

2 Samuel 12:1-5 (The poor man and his ewe lamb.)
D&C 46:32 (Give thanks for whatsoever blessing.)
D&C 59:16, 18 (Animals are given to gladden the heart.)
• How has our pet been a joy and a gift for our family?
• How can we thank God for this gift?
• How can we bid farewell to our pet?

B. God Is Mindful of Our Pet

Matthew 10:29 or *Luke 12:6* (Not one sparrow is forgotten by God.)
D&C 45:1 (The Lord made all things which live.)
Moses 1:53 (All things are mine, and I know them.)
• What do these passages teach us about the value of an animal's life?
• What difference does it make to realize that God knows our pet?
• What do we imagine the Savior would say if he were here now?

C. Animals and the Afterlife

Revelation 5:11-14 (John saw animals praising God in heaven.)
D&C 77:2-4 (Animals enjoy eternal felicity.)
D&C 130:2 (That same sociality which exists here will exist there.)
• What difference does it make to know that animals also live after death?
• What might D&C 130:2 suggest about our relationship with our pet?
• How do we imagine our pet giving praise to God?

D. An End to Pain

Revelation 20:4 (Neither shall there be any more pain.)
Alma 40:12 (Paradise is a state of rest and peace.)

D&C 104:11-13 (We are accountable to God for our steward-ships.)

• How must our Heavenly Father feel to see one of his creatures suffer?

• To what extent do promises of rest in the afterlife apply to animals as well as human beings?

• How is ending our pet's suffering an act of responsible stewardship?

Discussions and Activities

A. Read Psalms 104 in its entirety. Discuss the questions: What do we learn from this psalm about God's love for all living things? What difference does that knowledge make in the face of our pet's death?

B. Read Psalms 145:14-16. Invite each family member to create a picture of the Savior caring for your pet, perhaps modeled after paintings of Jesus as the Good Shepherd.

C. As a family, create a drawing or collage to depict the whole creation worshiping God, as described in Revelation 5:11-14. Include your pet among the worshiping creatures.

D. Explain that when Heavenly Father created the world, he decreed that every living thing should fulfill the measure of its creation and have joy therein, Abraham 4:20-25 could provide the starting point for this discussion. Invite family members to comment on the questions: How did our pet fulfill the measure of its creation? In what ways did our pet experience joy?

E. Offer a prayer thanking God for the gift of your pet and commending your pet into God's hands. If you bury your pet, it would be especially appropriate to offer this prayer at the burial spot.

Illness or Disability

Songs and Hymns

Heavenly Father, Now I Pray (*Children's Songbook* 19)
I'll Walk with You (*Children's Songbook* 140)
Every Star is Different (*Children's Songbook* 142)
I Need Thee Every Hour (*Hymns* 98)

Nearer, My God, to Thee (*Hymns* 100)
Cast Thy Burden upon the Lord (*Hymns* 110)
Come, Ye Disconsolate (*Hymns* 115)
Be Still, My Soul (*Hymns* 124)
Children of Our Heavenly Father (*Hymns* 299)
I Am a Child of God (*Hymns* 301, *Children's Songbook* 2)

Lesson Ideas

A. Blessing the Sick

Mark 6:7, 12-13 (Jesus sent the twelve to anoint the sick with oil.)

James 5:14 (Let the elders pray over the sick, anointing them with oil.)

D&C 42:43-44 (The elders shall lay hands upon the sick in my name.)

• According to D&C 42, what is the purpose of laying hands on the sick?

• How is receiving a health blessing like being blessed by the Savior himself?

• How does a health blessing serve as an expression of our concern for our loved one?

B. Caring for the Sick

Matthew 25:34-40 (I was sick and ye visited me.)

D&C 42:43 (Nourish the sick with all tenderness.)

D&C 52:40 (Remember the sick and the afflicted.)

• What special needs does our loved one have as a result of his/her condition?

• What would our loved one find helpful or comforting?

• How can we help nourish our loved one spiritually, as well as physically?

C. Sharing the Burden

Romans 15:1 (The strong ought to bear the infirmities of the weak.)

1 Corinthians 12:20-23, 26 (If one member suffer, all suffer with it.)

Mosiah 18:8-10 (Ye are willing to bear one another's burdens.)

• How does our loved one's condition place new burdens on all family members?

- What adjustments do we need to make in order to cope with these burdens?
- How can we each preserve our physical and spiritual strength?

D. God Is My Support

Isaiah 40:28-29 (He giveth power to the faint.)
Alma 37:36-37 (Cry unto God for all thy support.)
D&C 24:8 (Be patient in afflictions, for I am with thee.)

- What new challenges does our loved one face as a result of his/her condition?
- Why is it important for our loved one to be patient as he/she learns to adapt?
- How can we be instruments of God in helping to support our loved one?

E. Thou Art with Me

Psalms 23:1-4 (In the valley of the shadow of death, thou art with me.)
2 Corinthians 1:3-5 (Our consolation aboundeth by Christ.)
D&C 88:4-6 (Christ is in all and through all.)

- In what sense is our loved one walking in the valley of the shadow of death?
- What difference does it make to know that Christ is with our loved one, no matter how bad things get?
- How can we be instruments of God in comforting our loved one?

F. Touched with Our Infirmities

Hebrews 4:15-16 (Christ is touched with the feeling of our infirmities.)
Alma 7:11-12 (He will take upon him our pains and sicknesses.)
D&C 133:52-53 (In all their afflictions, he was afflicted.)

- What difference does it make to know that Christ suffers with our loved one?
- When has our loved one received "grace to help in time of need" (Hebrews 4:16)?
- In what sense do we feel that God is "carrying" our loved one (D&C 133:53)?

G. How Long, O Lord?

Romans 8:22-26 (We groan within ourselves, waiting.)

2 Nephi 31:19-20 (Ye must press forward with steadfastness.)

D&C 24:8 (Be patient in afflictions, for I am with thee.)

• How can we preserve hope and patience in the face of our loved one's condition?

• What difference does it make to know that God is with us?

• What would it mean, in our circumstances, to rely wholly on Christ (2 Nephi 31:19)?

H. An Optimistic Spirit

Proverbs 18:14 (The spirit of a man will sustain his infirmity.)

Alma 33:23 (May your burdens be light through the joy of God's Son.)

D&C 68:6 (Be of good cheer, for I will stand by you.)

• How does an optimistic attitude contribute to a person's health?

• What is the difference between optimism and denial?

• How can our loved one's relationship with the Savior help him/her retain an optimistic outlook?

I. Thy Will Be Done

Matthew 26:39 (Not as I will, but as thou wilt.)

Romans 8:26-28 (All things work for the good of them that love God.)

D&C 46:30-32 (Whoso asketh in the Spirit asketh according to God's will.)

• What would we will for our loved one if we could?

• Why is it hard to distinguish the Spirit's promptings from our own hopes, wishes, and fears?

• How can we find the strength to accept God's will if it does not match our own?

J. The Gift of Healing

2 Corinthians 12:7-9 (Paul prayed unsuccessfully for relief.)

Moroni 10:8-17 (The gift of healing comes according as God wills.)

D&C 46:10-12, 19-20 (All have not every gift given unto them.)

• What do we learn from these passages about why some people seem to experience miracles and others do not?

- What does it mean to say God's grace is sufficient for our loved one (2 Corinthians 12:9)?
- What healing might a person receive other than being cured of a physical ailment?

K. The Gift of Medicine

Matthew 4:23-24 (Jesus healed all manner of sickness.)

Alma 46:40 (God prepared means to remove the cause of diseases.)

D&C 59:18-19 (Things of the earth are to strengthen the body.)

- In what sense do health workers carry out the work of Jesus?
- In what sense do medical researchers receive revelation?
- What treatments, or methods of coping, has God provided for our loved one's condition?

Discussions and Activities

A. Read 1 Kings 17:17-18. Discuss the following questions: Why is it normal for a person to react to a serious illness or disability with anger or depression? How can a person progress beyond these feelings?

B. Read or recount the story of the invalid lowered to Jesus through the roof (Mark 2:1-5). Note the important part played in this man's healing by the four friends who carried his bed. Discuss the questions: What kind of people must these have been to go to such lengths on behalf of a sick friend? How can we show that kind of concern for our loved one?

C. Ask each family member to copy out at least one scripture which they feel could provide comfort, assurance, or hope to your loved one. Then ask each family member to create an illustration to accompany each scripture he/she chose. Bind the scriptures and illustrations together into a booklet, as a gift for your loved one.

D. In the case of a loved one with a chronic illness or disability, read D&C 4:1-3. Ask family members to brainstorm a list of talents, gifts, or personality traits which your loved one can use to serve God and others despite his/her illness or disability. Discuss the question: How does service make our lives more meaningful and satisfying?

E. In the case of a loved one with a disability, read Genesis 1:27 (Moses 2:27). Discuss the question: What difference does it make to realize that, disability and all, our loved one is in the image of God?

F. Read 1 Corinthians 12:18-22. Note that every member of your family faces certain challenges or difficulties, at the same time that every member of your family makes certain contributions to the family's well-being.

G. Read 1 Corinthians 12:22-23 and D&C 18:10. Discuss the questions: How might people react negatively to our loved one because of his/her condition? Why do people react this way? What can we do to show others how important our loved one is to us and to help them feel more comfortable around our loved one?

H. Depending on the circumstances of your loved one's illness or disability, some of the ideas which appear in the section of this book titled "Loss of a Dream" may be applicable.

I. Seek the Spirit's guidance in deciding how much information to give children about a loved one's condition. You may find the following scriptures applicable: 1 Corinthians 3:2; D&C 131:6; 2 Nephi 28:30; and D&C 100:5-6.

J. When taking children to visit a sick loved one, prepare them for the experience by explaining what they will see, hear, smell, and so on. Discuss with the children what they should do or say during the visit, preferably in terms of "do's" rather than "do not's."

K. Following a successful surgery or recovery, read Psalms 30:1-4. Make a thanksgiving offering of time or money to a worthy cause.

L. Consider doing the following in the closing prayer (especially if you used the lesson, "The Gift of Medicine").

• Give thanks for the medical knowledge and technology which have helped your loved one.

• Give thanks for the service rendered by health professionals of different kinds.

• Ask that the health workers who attend your loved one will be blessed with insight.

• Pray for continued advances in medicine.

Ideas for a Health Blessing

Preparation on the part of all participants can make a health blessing a powerful spiritual experience. Consider the following suggestions.

A. The one who has requested the blessing may want to read D&C 42:44 and reflect on the following questions: How is receiving a health blessing an act of trust in God's will? How can I prepare myself to discern and accept God's will for me?

At the same time, those who are going to administer the blessing may want to read D&C 42:44 and reflect on the following questions: What do I feel inspired to "pray for" on behalf of my loved one? How can I seek the Spirit's direction in deciding what the purpose of this health blessing ought to be?

B. Those who are going to administer the blessing might consider meeting beforehand with the person who has requested the blessing to discuss questions such as the following:

• What prompted the person to request the blessing?

• How does he/she hope to be benefitted by receiving the blessing?

• What concerns or anxieties does he/she have about his/her condition?

Having this information can help those who will administer the blessing seek inspiration from the Spirit (see D&C 9:7-8).

C. Family members might consider fasting together with those who are going to administer the blessing.

D. Treat the health blessing like a short devotional. Open with a song and a prayer. Pray that the Savior will be present and that all in attendance will be attentive to the Spirit.

E. Review the purpose of a health blessing, perhaps using Lesson Idea A, above.

F. Before administering the blessing, give each family member a chance to express their own concerns or hopes regarding the one who is to be blessed. As you perform the blessing, try to discern what the Spirit may have to say in response to family members' concerns and hopes.

G. Following the blessing, sing another hymn to conclude the devotional. (A closing prayer would probably be redundant, but follow the promptings of the Spirit on this point.)

Depression

Songs and Hymns

Heavenly Father, Now I Pray (*Children's Songbook* 19)
God's Love (*Children's Songbook* 97)
I Need Thee Every Hour (*Hymns* 98)
Cast Thy Burden upon the Lord (*Hymns* 110)
Come, Ye Disconsolate (*Hymns* 115)
Be Still, My Soul (*Hymns* 124)
Where Can I Turn for Peace? (*Hymns* 129)
Abide With Me! (*Hymns* 166)
I Am a Child of God (*Hymns* 301, *Children's Songbook* 2)

Lesson Ideas

A. Supporting Our Loved One

Matthew 25:34-40 (I was sick and ye visited me.)
D&C 42:43 (Nourish the sick with all tenderness.)
D&C 52:40 (Remember the sick and the afflicted.)

• What difference does it make to realize that our loved one is ill, not just "down"?

• How can we support our loved one as he/she learns to cope with depression?

• At the same time, how can we preserve our own emotional well-being?

B. Sharing the Burden

Romans 15:1 (The strong ought to bear the infirmities of the weak.)
1 Corinthians 12:20-23, 26 (If one member suffer, all suffer with it.)
Mosiah 18:8-10 (Willing to bear one another's burdens.)

• How does our loved one's depression place new burdens on all family members?

• What adjustments do we need to make in order to cope with these burdens?

• How can we each preserve our own physical and spiritual strength?

C. Means to Cope

Matthew 4:23-24 (Jesus healed all manner of sickness.)
Alma 46:40 (God prepared means to remove the cause of diseases.)
D&C 59:18-19 (Things of the earth are to strengthen the body.)
• What treatments or therapies are available to help our loved one?
• How can we express our gratitude to God for making these treatments available?
• In what sense could it be said that the professionals helping our loved one are doing the Savior's work?

D. Thou Art with Me

Psalms 23:1-4 (I walk through the valley of the shadow of death.)
D&C 88:4-6 (Christ is in all and through all.)
D&C 133:52-53 (In all their afflictions, he was afflicted.)
• In what sense is our loved one walking in the valley of the shadow of death?
• What difference does it make to know that Christ shares our loved one's suffering?
• What difference does it make to know that Christ is with our loved one, no matter what happens?

E. How Long, O Lord?

Romans 8:22-26 (We groan within ourselves, waiting.)
2 Nephi 31:19-20 (Press forward with steadfastness.)
D&C 24:8 (Be patient in afflictions, for I am with thee.)
• How can we preserve hope and patience in the face of our loved one's depression?
• What difference does it make to know that God is with us in adversity?
• What would it mean, in our circumstances, to rely wholly on Christ (2 Nephi 31:19)?

F. Every Hair Is Numbered

Matthew 10:29-31 (The very hairs of your head are all numbered.)

Luke 15:3-6 (The Good Shepherd goes out to find the lost sheep.)

D&C 18:10 (Remember the worth of souls is great in God's sight.)

- What difference does it make to know that God is watching over our loved one?

- In what sense is our loved one like the lost sheep in the parable?

- How can we let our loved one know how much we care about him/her?

Discussions and Activities

A. Encourage your loved one to seek professional help for his/her depression. It is especially important to seek help if your loved one is suicidal. Various kinds of treatment are available for depression, depending on the circumstances. Seek the Spirit's guidance in deciding how best to help your loved one. You may find it helpful to read the article, "Why Is My Wife (or Husband) Depressed?" *Ensign*, Mar. 1990, pp. 27-29.

B. Read or retell the story of Hannah praying in the temple (1 Samuel 1). Apply the story to your loved one's depression by discussing the following sets of questions:

1. Why was Elkanah unable to comfort Hannah (v. 8)? What clichés do people today use when trying to comfort someone suffering from depression? Why are those clichés not really helpful?

2. Why did Eli react so negatively to Hannah at first (v. 14)? Why might people today react negatively to someone with depression?

3. What finally brought comfort to Hannah (vv. 17-18)? How can we support our loved one as he/she copes with depression?

C. Consider the passages of scripture in the list below. Reflect on the question: What difference does it make to know that people from the scriptures—including the Savior— experienced depression or despair?

- Job 3:11-13 (Why died I not from the womb?)
- Job 6:2-3 (My grief is heavier than the sands of the sea.)
- Psalms 10:1 (Lord, why hidest thou in times of trouble?)

- Psalms 13:1-3 (Hear me, Lord, lest I sleep the sleep of death.)
- Psalms 22:1-2 (My God, why hast thou forsaken me?)
- Psalms 69:20 (I looked for comforters, but I found none.)
- Isaiah 53:3 or Mosiah 14:3 (A man of sorrows.)
- Jeremiah 20:14, 18 (Cursed be the day wherein I was born.)
- Matthew 27:46 or Mark 15:34 (Jesus despaired on the cross.)
- 2 Corinthians 1:8 (We despaired even of life.)
- 2 Nephi 4:17-18 (My heart sorroweth; I am encompassed about.)
- Alma 8:14 (Wading through much tribulation and anguish.)
- JS-H 1:15-16 (I was ready to abandon myself to destruction.)

D. Read Alma 15:1-11. Discuss the questions: How is it that guilt can cause a person to become ill? How can an understanding of the atonement help people resist this kind of guilt? In what sense could it be said that the gospel of Jesus Christ is "anti-guilt"?

E. Read Matthew 5:48 (3 Nephi 12:48). Discuss the questions: How might someone prone to depression find this passage devastating? How should we understand this passage? Ask family members to identify additional passages of scriptures which might be devastating if taken the wrong way. What is the key to taking these passages the right way?

F. Ask each family member to come to the devotional with a passage of scripture, or a quotation from a General Authority, which reaffirms the unconditional love of our Savior or our Heavenly Father. Have each family member create a drawing, painting, or collage to illustrate the passage he/she chose. Bind the scriptures and illustrations together into a booklet, as a gift for your loved one.

G. Read Matthew 11:28-30. Discuss the question: What consolation does this passage offer someone coping with depression?

H. Invite family members to recount times in their lives when they felt that God helped them overcome adversity. Then read 2 Corinthians 1:8-10. Note that Paul links the power to overcome adversity to Christ's resurrection. The same power by which Christ overcame death is available to help us overcome everything that threatens us or keeps us from developing our full potential. Discuss the question: How does this principle relate to coping with depression (either your own or a loved one's)?

I. Family members may feel guilty or helpless because they are unable to make their loved one "better." They may feel that if they were a better parent, spouse, etc., their loved one wouldn't be so depressed. Read Helaman 12:7 and Moses 1:10. Reflect in your journal on the questions: How has my loved one's depression forced me to recognize my limitations? How can I trust God to do for my loved one what I cannot?

J. Seek the Spirit's guidance in deciding how much information to give children about your loved one's depression. You may find the following scriptures applicable: 1 Corinthians 3:2; D&C 131:6; 2 Nephi 28:30; and D&C 100:5-6.

K. If you have a loved one who is suicidal, read Luke 23:46. Reflect on the question: What would it mean, in these circumstances, for me to commend my loved one to God?

L. If a loved one is suicidal, family members may be wise to prepare for the worst. Will family members know what to do if the loved one makes a suicide attempt? Will they recognize the warning signs? Will they know how to get help? Individual discussions with each family member may be the best way to broach this topic. The scriptural promise, "If ye are prepared ye shall not fear" (D&C 38:30) could set the tone for this discussion.

M. Encourage your loved one to write often in his/her journal, as a way of expressing and coming to terms with negative feelings. Other family members might find this helpful as well.

N. In the spirit of the injunction to "seek learning, even by study" (D&C 88:118), encourage family members to educate themselves about depression. Invite family members to share what they have learned in subsequent devotionals.

O. Consider concluding the devotional with a health blessing for your loved one, in lieu of a closing prayer. (See "Ideas for a Health Blessing," in the section of this book titled "Illness or Disability.") Family members seeking added strength to cope with a loved one's depression may also find it helpful to receive a priesthood blessing.

Addiction

Note: As used here, the word "addiction" is meant to refer not only to substance abuse, but also to other compulsive behaviors such as eating disorders.

Songs and Hymns

A Mighty Fortress Is Our God (*Hymns* 68)
Press Forward, Saints (*Hymns* 81)
How Firm a Foundation (*Hymns* 85)
I Need Thee Every Hour (*Hymns* 98)
Jesus, Savior, Pilot Me (*Hymns* 104)
Be Still, My Soul (*Hymns* 124)
Where Can I Turn for Peace? (*Hymns* 129)
I Know that My Redeemer Lives (*Hymns* 136)
I Am a Child of God (*Hymns* 301, *Children's Songbook* 2)

Lesson Ideas

A. Seeking Help and Guidance

Exodus 18:18 (This thing is too heavy for thee alone.)
Proverbs 15:22 (Without counsel purposes are disappointed.)
Alma 37:37 (Counsel with the Lord; he will direct thee.)

• Why is it important—and difficult—to seek outside help in coping with addiction?

• How can we seek the Lord's guidance in deciding where to turn for help?

• To what degree do other family members need help and support, not just the one who is addicted?

B. Christ Shares Our Afflictions

Alma 7:11-12 (He will take upon him our infirmities.)
D&C 88:4-6 (Christ is in all and through all.)
D&C 133:52-53 (In all their afflictions, he was afflicted.)

• How is Christ able to know what it is like to cope with addiction?

• What does it mean to say that Christ shares all our afflictions?

• What difference does it make to know that he is with us, no matter how difficult things get?

C. God Delivers from Bondage

Leviticus 26:13 (I have broken the bands of your yoke.)

Luke 4:16-21 (Christ came to set captives free.)

Alma 36:2 (They were in bondage; God did deliver them.)

• What stories from the scriptures show God bringing deliverance from bondage?

• How might these stories be applied to addiction?

• What steps can we take to draw on Christ's power to deliver?

D. With God Nothing Is Impossible

Luke 1:37 (With God nothing is impossible.)

Philippians 4:13 (I can do all things through Christ.)

Ether 12:27 (I will make weak things become strong unto you.)

• How can we draw on Christ's power in coping with addiction?

• Why does change not happen as quickly or easily as we might wish?

• What is the difference between relying on God and expecting a "miracle cure"?

E. Newness of Life

Romans 6:3-6 (That we should walk in newness of life.)

Mosiah 27:22-29 (Alma became a new creature through God's grace.)

D&C 29:24 (Old things shall pass away; all shall become new.)

• Why does coping with addiction involve changing one's whole way of life?

• In what sense could it be said that learning to cope with addiction is a kind of transfiguration or resurrection?

• How can we draw on the power of the atonement in coping with addiction?

F. Living with Joy

Isaiah 51:11 or *2 Nephi 8:11* (The redeemed shall obtain joy.)

John 15:11 (These things have I spoken that your joy might be full.)

2 Nephi 2:25 (Men are that they might have joy.)

- In what sense is learning to live with joy the key to coping with addiction?
- What has Christ taught us about how to live with joy?
- When have we experienced joy? How can we cultivate more such experiences?

G. One Day at a Time

Psalms 37:23-24 (Your steps are ordered by the Lord.)

Matthew 6:26-34 or *3 Nephi 13:26-34* (Take no thought for the morrow.)

D&C 58:3 (Ye cannot behold for now the design of your God.)

- What does it mean to take things one day at a time?
- How can living one day at a time help people cope with addiction?
- What difference does it make to know that God is ordering our steps, even if we cannot see it now?

H. The Worth of a Soul

Jeremiah 31:3 (I have loved thee with an everlasting love.)

2 Nephi 26:25 (Doth he cry unto any: Depart from me?)

D&C 18:10 (The worth of souls is great in God's sight.)

- How can a knowledge of God's unconditional love help people who are coping with addiction?
- What would it mean for us to love one another unconditionally?
- What do we imagine the Savior would say if he were here now?

Discussions and Activities

A. If an addicted loved one refuses to acknowledge that he/she has a problem with addiction, read D&C 43:24. Reflect on the following questions, perhaps in your journal:

- How must Heavenly Father feel when his children make choices that result in their own harm? Why does he not keep them from doing so?
- Why is it important for me to recognize that I cannot force my loved one to change?
- Until my loved one is willing to face the problem, what steps can I take to preserve my own well-being and happiness? How can I continue to let my loved one know that I am concerned about him/her?

B. Family members may take steps to conceal a loved one's addiction. This shields the addict from the consequences of his/her behavior, thus making it easier for the addict to deny he/she has a problem. Read Luke 12:1-3. Reflect on the following questions: Why is secrecy an unhelpful response to addiction? What is the difference between respecting my loved one's privacy and abetting his/her addiction? Where could I appropriately turn for outside help?

C. Read Helaman 12:7 and Moses 1:10. Then do one of the following.

    1. If you yourself are struggling with addiction, reflect in your journal on the questions: Why is merely exercising willpower not going to solve my problem? How can I seek the Savior's help as I work through the process of making changes in my life?

    2. If you have a family member who is struggling with addiction, reflect in your journal on the questions: Why is it important to recognize that I cannot solve my loved one's problem? How can I trust the Savior to do for my loved one what I cannot?

D. There are multiple theories about how to cope with addiction and different kinds of resources available to help. Seek the Spirit's guidance in deciding how best to help yourself or your loved one.

E. Read D&C 93:43. Discuss the questions: To what degree is the loved one's addiction a family problem, not just an individual one? How can other family members (not just the addicted loved one) seek needed support?

F. Discuss the process of learning to cope with addiction. Emphasize that the process is slow and difficult, and that there may be relapses on the way. Then read 2 Nephi 31:19-20. Discuss the questions: How can we find the strength to push on when we feel overwhelmed or worn out? How should we react if a relapse occurs?

G. Make a list of the resources family members are using to cope with addiction (counseling, support groups, treatment programs, and so on). Then read 2 Nephi 25:23 and discuss the question: In addition to employing these other resources, how can family members open themselves to the Savior's grace?

H. Read 2 Corinthians 1:8-10. Note that Paul links the power to overcome adversity to Christ's resurrection. The same power by which Christ overcame death is available to help us overcome everything that threatens us or keeps us from developing our full potential. Discuss the question: How does this principle relate to coping with addiction (either your own or a loved one's)?

I. If family members are seeking help through a principles-based program (for example, a 12-step program), prepare a presentation on those principles. Identify connections between the principles of the program and principles of the restored gospel.

J. In the spirit of the injunction to "seek learning, even by study" (D&C 88:118), encourage family members to educate themselves about addiction. Invite family members to share what they have learned in subsequent devotionals.

K. Commit to remember your loved one regularly in your family and personal prayers.

L. Consider concluding the devotional with a health blessing for your loved one, in lieu of a closing prayer. (See "Ideas for a Health Blessing," in the section of this book titled "Illness or Disability.")

Victimization

Note: The term "victimization," as used here, could refer to a variety of crimes, ranging from vandalism, robbery, or fraud, to abuse, assault, or rape. Pick those devotional ideas which seem applicable to your situation.

Songs and Hymns

Heavenly Father, Now I Pray (*Children's Songbook* 19)
We Bow Our Heads (*Children's Songbook* 25)
God's Love (*Children's Songbook* 97)
How Firm a Foundation (*Hymns* 85)
The Lord Is My Light (*Hymns* 89)
I Need Thee Every Hour (*Hymns* 98)
Cast Thy Burden upon the Lord (*Hymns* 110)
Come, Ye Disconsolate (*Hymns* 115)
Be Still, My Soul (*Hymns* 124)
I Am a Child of God (*Hymns* 301, *Children's Songbook* 2)

Lesson Ideas
A. The Lord Shares Our Hurt
Isaiah 50:6 or *2 Nephi 7:6* (I gave my back to the smiters.)
Matthew 27:26-35 (Jesus was mocked, abused, and crucified.)
Alma 7:11-12 (He will take upon him our pains.)
• When we have been hurt or victimized, what difference does it make to know that Christ also suffered victimization?
• According to Alma, why did the Savior suffer the things he did?
• How can we seek the Lord's "succor" (Alma 7:12)?

B. God Is Our Refuge
Psalms 3:2-5 (Thou, O Lord, art a shield for me.)
Psalms 71:1-4 (Thou art my rock and my fortress.)
Isaiah 54:14 or *3 Nephi 22:14* (Oppression and terror shall be far from thee.)
• What does it mean to say that God is "the lifter up of mine head" (Psalms 3:3)?
• What difference does it make to know we can "continually resort" to God (Psalms 71:3)?
• In what sense can God put our hurt far from us?

C. God Will Heal
Psalms 147:3 (He healeth the broken in heart.)
Malachi 4:2 or *3 Nephi 25:2* (The Son shall arise with healing in his wings.)
Matthew 4:23-24 (Jesus healed all manner of torments.)
• What different kinds of healing do members of our family need?
• In what sense do both victimizers and victimized need healing?
• How can the Savior help us heal?

D. Our Divine Worth
Psalms 118:5-6 (The Lord is on my side.)
Matthew 10:29-31 (Fear not; the hairs of your head are all numbered.)
D&C 18:10 (Remember the worth of souls is great in God's sight.)
• How can being victimized cause a person to doubt his/her worth?

• What difference does it make to realize how much we are worth in God's eyes?

• What do we imagine Heavenly Father would say now if he were here?

E. Overcoming Fear
Psalms 56:3-4 (When I am afraid, I will trust in thee.)
2 Timothy 1:7 (God hath not given us the spirit of fear.)
D&C 6:36 (Look unto me in every thought; fear not.)
• Why is it important that we not allow others to make us afraid?
• What is the difference between fear and prudent caution?
• How can trust in God help us overcome fear?

F. Overcoming Bitterness
Matthew 5:43-45 or *3 Nephi 12:43-45* (Love your enemies.)
4 Nephi 1:34 (The people of Jesus did not smite again.)
D&C 98:23-26 (Revile not against them, neither seek revenge.)
• Why is it important not to respond to hatred and violence with more of the same?
• How can we bring ourselves to forgive those who have hurt us?
• What is the difference between seeking revenge and seeking justice?

Discussions and Activities
A. Read Isaiah 60:18. Discuss the questions: Why is it important that we not simply "put up with" victimization? What steps can we take to put an end to the victimization of our family member(s)?

B. Read Psalms 18:6-8, 16-19. Discuss the question: How must God feel about what has happened to our family member(s)?

C. Read Psalms 109 and discuss the question: Why is anger a natural, response to being hurt (or to seeing someone we love be hurt)? Then read 2 Nephi 4:26-30 and discuss the question: Why is it important that we learn to let go of anger?

D. Read Mosiah 18:8-10. Discuss the questions: What would it mean for us to mourn what has happened with one another? How can we comfort one another?

E. Read Job 2:11-13. Discuss the questions: Why do people often feel uncomfortable around someone who is experiencing strong emotions? How can we show our support for someone who is hurting if we do not know what to say?

F. Invite each family member to create a drawing or collage depicting his/her feelings about what has happened. After the drawings are complete, read and discuss Psalms 4:1. Have each family member title his/her drawing, "Hear me when I call, O God." Invite family members to hang their drawings near their beds, where they will see them during personal prayers.

G. As part of the lesson, "Overcoming Fear," gather around a lighted candle and read Psalms 27:1. Invite each family member to express their thoughts and feelings in response to the question: When has my faith in the Lord helped me overcome fear?

H. As part of the lesson, "Overcoming Bitterness," suggest that family members remember in their personal prayers not only the victimized, but also the victimizer. Emphasize that family members are free to decide for themselves whether praying for the victimizer is something they feel they can do at this point in their lives. Moroni 7:48 might prove useful for this discussion.

I. Someone who has been victimized may find the Book of Psalms particularly meaningful for study, since many of the psalms were written in response to hurts inflicted by others.

J. Seek the Spirit's guidance in deciding how much information to give children about the victimization a loved one has suffered, especially in a case of sexual abuse or sexual assault. You may find the following scriptures applicable: 1 Corinthians 3:2; D&C 131:6; 2 Nephi 28:30; and D&C 100:5-6.

K. In the case of a loved one who has suffered abuse or assault, read D&C 109:48. Then reflect in your journal on the following questions: To what extent might this verse be a description of my loved one? What burdens does my loved one bear as a result of the abuse he/she has suffered? How do I feel about what has happened to my loved one? How can I let my heart "flow out" to my loved one?

L. We live in a society that is accustomed to speak of "moral cleanliness." One unfortunate consequence of this is that people who have been the victims of sexual abuse or sexual assault may perceive themselves, and may unconsciously be perceived by others, as "unclean" or "defiled." Discuss the question: What difference does it make to understand that when we talk about moral cleanliness, what we mean is moral responsibility?

M. Find out what resources are available to help family members cope with what has happened. These might include crisis intervention, counseling, support groups, legal assistance services, or victims rights advocates.

N. Get involved in a group that combats victimization—for instance, a neighborhood watch program, a support organization, or a crisis center. Active involvement in a cause can help someone who has been victimized feel more empowered (see D&C 58:27-28).

O. Discuss steps that family members can take to help prevent future victimization. At the same time, be sure to emphasize that victimization is never the victim's "fault"—it is the victimizer who is guilty of wrong-doing.

P. In a case where your home has been violated (vandalism, break-in, domestic abuse), you might find it comforting to rededicate your home. See "Ideas for a Home Dedication," in the section of this book titled "Moving."

Q. Family members in need of either physical or emotional healing may want to receive a health blessing. See "Ideas for a Health Blessing," in the section of this book titled "Illness or Disability."

Disaster

Songs and Hymns

For Health and Strength (*Children's Songbook* 21)
For Thy Bounteous Blessings (*Children's Songbook* 21)
Come, Come, Ye Saints (*Hymns* 30)
How Firm a Foundation (*Hymns* 85)
I Need Thee Every Hour (*Hymns* 98)
Nearer, My God, to Thee (*Hymns* 100)
Cast Thy Burden upon the Lord (*Hymns* 110)
Come, Ye Disconsolate (*Hymns* 115)
Be Still, My Soul (*Hymns* 124)
Children of Our Heavenly Father (*Hymns* 299)

Lesson Ideas

A. God Shares our Sorrows

Isaiah 53:3-4 or *Mosiah 14:3-4* (Surely he has borne our griefs.)

Alma 7:11-12 (He will take upon him the pains of his people.)

D&C 133:52-53 (In all their afflictions he was afflicted.)

• What have we lost as a result of this disaster?

• What difference does it make to know that God mourns our loss with us?

• In what sense is God "carrying" us (D&C 133:53)?

B. God Will Help Us

Isaiah 41:10 (Fear not, I will help thee.)

Matthew 6:25-26, 34 (Heavenly Father will provide for your needs.)

Mosiah 24:15 (The Lord strengthened the people to bear their burdens.)

• How does trusting in God's care help us find peace of mind?

• How can we draw on God's strength as we face the aftermath of this disaster?

• How can we help each other be patient (see Mosiah 24:15)?

C. Keeping Faith Alive

Psalms 42:11 (Why art thou cast down, O my soul?)

2 Nephi 31:19-20 (Press forward with a perfect brightness of hope.)

Moroni 10:23 (If ye have faith ye can do all things which are expedient.)

• How has this disaster been a trial to our faith?

• How can we strengthen our faith to face the challenges ahead?

• How can we help lift each other's spirits?

D. Giving Thanks for Our Blessings

1 Thessalonians 5:18 (In every thing give thanks.)

3 Nephi 10:9-10 (The people's mourning turned into thanksgiving.)

D&C 98:1-3 (Your afflictions shall work together for your good.)

• How might things have been worse than they actually were?

• How have we been blessed in the aftermath of the disaster?

• How can we find it in ourselves to give thanks in the midst of loss?

E. The Things That Matter Most

Ecclesiastes 2:4-11 (All the works I had wrought were vanity.)
Matthew 6:19-20 or *3 Nephi 13:19-20* (Lay up treasures in heaven.)
Luke 10:41-42 (But one thing is needful.)
• Why is it natural to grieve the loss of material possessions?
• What have we learned during this experience about the things that matter most?
• What does our family have that no disaster can ever take away from us?

F. We Will Rebuild

Isaiah 61:4 (They shall raise up the former desolations.)
Nehemiah 2:17-18 (The Jews rebuilt Jerusalem.)
4 Nephi 1:7-9 (The Nephites rebuilt their cities.)
• What difference does it make to know that the Lord's people in the past successfully rebuilt after disaster?
• Why does God desire that "waste places" be built back up?
• How can we "strengthen our hands" for the work ahead?

G. Helping Hearts and Hands

Galatians 6:2 (Bear ye one another's burdens.)
Alma 15:18 (Alma administered to Amulek in his tribulations.)
D&C 42:33 (Church members should administer to others.)
• What aid have we received in the aftermath of the disaster?
• How can we help administer to the needs of others, both now and in the future?
• How has this disaster brought people together?

Discussions and Activities

A. Read Psalms 22:1-2 and Matthew 27:46. Discuss the question: At times when it seems that God has failed or abandoned us, what difference does it make to know that Jesus felt this way also?

B. In the case of a family who has lost their home, read Luke 9:57-58. Discuss the question: What difference does it make to realize that Jesus also knew what it was like to be without a home?

C. Point out how often in the early days of the restored church the Saints had to start over after losing their homes and other possessions. Discuss the question: Where did the Saints find the strength to go on rebuilding in the face of disaster? How can our family draw on that same strength?

D. Review the scriptural promise, "If ye are prepared ye shall not fear" (D&C 38:30). Discuss how advanced preparations on the part of your family, the Church, government agencies, and so on, have helped you get through this disaster.

E. Once you are in a position to do so, express your gratitude for the aid you received during the disaster by making a thanksgiving offering—an especially generous fast offering, for example, or a contribution to the Church's humanitarian fund.

F. As a family, observe the anniversary of the disaster each year with a special meal—a kind of miniature Thanksgiving—to remind you of how you were blessed and helped. For instance, you might on this day prepare a meal entirely from food storage.

G. If your home needs to be repaired or rebuilt, you might find it meaningful to rededicate your home once the work is complete. See "Ideas for a Home Dedication," in the section of this book titled "Moving."

Moving

Songs and Hymns

This Is God's House (*Children's Songbook* 30)
Home (*Children's Songbook* 192)
When We're Helping (*Children's Songbook* 198)
The Wise Man and the Foolish Man (*Children's Songbook* 281)
God Be With You Till We Meet Again (*Hymns* 152)
Abide With Me; 'Tis Eventide (*Hymns* 165)
This House We Dedicate to Thee (*Hymns* 245)
Love at Home (*Hymns* 294)
Home Can Be a Heaven on Earth (*Hymns* 298)

Lesson Ideas

A. Preparing for the Move

Matthew 9:37 (The work is great, the laborers are few.)
Mosiah 4:27 (See that all things are done in wisdom and order.)
D&C 101:68 (Let all things be prepared before you.)
- What needs to be done in preparation for our move?
- How can we keep from being overwhelmed by everything that needs doing?
- How can we divide up tasks among the members of our family?

B. Saying Goodbye

Genesis 12:1, 4-5 or *Abraham 2:3-4* (Abraham's family left their old home.)
1 Nephi 2:2-4 (Lehi's family left their old home.)
JS-H 1:3-4 (Joseph Smith's family moved from place to place.)
- How do you imagine these families must have felt about leaving their homes?
- Whom and what will we be leaving behind when we move?
- How might we bid farewell to the people and places we love?

C. Protected in Our Travels

Exodus 13:21-22 (A pillar of cloud and fire went before the Israelites.)
Ether 6:4-7 (The Jaredites commended themselves to the Lord.)
D&C 49:27 (I will go before you and be your rearward.)
- How did the Lord help the Israelites and the Jaredites in their travels?
- What would it mean for us to commend ourselves to the Lord?
- How does knowing that God is with us help ease the stress of moving?

D. Making a New Start

1 Nephi 18:23-25 (The Nephites set up their new home.)
Mosiah 23:1-5 (The people of Alma set up their new home.)
Ether 6:11-13 (The Jaredites set up their new home.)
- What do we have to give thanks for as we end our travels?
- What work needs to be done to get us settled in our new home?
- What do we have to look forward to in this new place?

E. Strangers in a Strange Place

Exodus 2:21-22 (I have been a stranger in a strange land.)

Matthew 25:34-40 (I was a stranger, and ye took me in.)

Alma 26:36-37 (God is mindful of us, wanderers in a strange land.)

• What difference does it make to know that God is with us in this new place?

• What have people done to help us feel welcome and more at ease here?

• What have we learned from this experience about how we could make others feel welcome in the future?

F. Inviting God into Our New Home

Zechariah 2:10 (I will dwell in the midst of thee.)

Luke 24:28-29 (He went in to tarry with them.)

D&C 88:119 (Establish a house of God.)

• How can we invite the Savior's presence into our new home?

• What would it mean for our new home to be a house of God?

• As we make this new start, what goals can we set to strengthen our family?

Discussions and Activities

A. Before moving preparations have become too hectic, spend an evening making farewell notes to give to friends or family members you will be leaving behind when you move.

B. Before leaving your old home, suggest that each family member invite their closest friends for a very simple farewell supper (for example, soup and crackers), or a potluck picnic in a favorite locale.

C. Create a drawing or collage of your family en route to your new home. Immediately over your vehicle, draw a bright cloud to represent God watching over your family. Leave plenty of space above the cloud. In that space, ask family members to write down worries or anxieties they have about the trip to your new home, or about settling into your new home. When you've finished the drawing, it should look as if the cloud is shielding your family from these worries and anxieties. Read Abraham 2:16 and discuss the question: How can trust in God help us confront our anxieties?

D. On the night before you move, invite family members to express thanks for things they will miss about their old home ("I'm thankful for . . ."). You might follow this up by inviting family members to express their hopes for the new home ("I'm looking forward to . . .").

E. Start your journey to your new home by reading any of the scriptures listed in the lesson, "Protected in Our Travels," and then offering a family prayer.

F. As you begin to settle into your new home, read D&C 57 in its entirety. Note how the Lord provided the Saints with specific direction about settling into their new home in Missouri. Discuss the question: How can our family seek the Lord's direction as we make our own new start in this new place?

G. Family members who are feeling particularly overwhelmed or anxious about the move might find it helpful to receive a priesthood blessing.

Ideas for a Home Dedication

According to the guidelines for performing priesthood ordinances prepared by the First Presidency, a person "need not hold the priesthood to dedicate a home because this is not a priesthood ordinance" (Melchizedek Priesthood Personal Study Guide, 1994 ed., p. 143). Strictly speaking, a home dedication is regarded as a special kind of "prayer," not a "blessing." The First Presidency guidelines also specify that a home need not be paid for before it is dedicated.

Consider the following suggestions for a special devotional to dedicate your new home.

A. Open with song and a brief prayer. In the prayer, thank God for having brought your family safely to your new home.

B. Read any of the following passages of scripture:

• Psalms 127:1 (Except the Lord build the house, they labour in vain.)

• Isaiah 12:4-6 or 2 Nephi 22:4-6 (Great is the Holy One in the midst of thee.)

• Matthew 7:24-25 or 3 Nephi 14:24-25 (A wise man built his house on a rock.)

• D&C 29:5-6 (Be glad, for I am in your midst.)

C. Have a family member present a brief talk or lesson on "Inviting God into Our New Home" (see Lesson Idea F, above).

D. Explain or review the purpose of a home dedication.

E. Before dedicating the home, give family members the opportunity to voice their individual hopes or wishes for your family's life in your new home.

F. Dedicate the home.

G. Close with another song. (A closing prayer would probably be redundant, but follow the promptings of the Spirit on this point.)

Financial Difficulties

Songs and Hymns

For Health and Strength (*Children's Songbook* 21)
Sing Your Way Home (*Children's Songbook* 193)
Lead, Kindly Light (*Hymns* 97)
I Need Thee Every Hour (*Hymns* 98)
Jesus, Savior, Pilot Me (*Hymns* 104)
Master, the Tempest Is Raging (*Hymns* 105)
Cast Thy Burden upon the Lord (*Hymns* 110)
When Faith Endures (*Hymns* 128)
Count Your Blessings (*Hymns* 241)

Lesson Ideas

A. Trust in God

Psalms 50:15 (Call upon me in the day of trouble.)

Matthew 7:7-11 or *3 Nephi 14:7-11* (Ask and it shall be given unto you.)

Philippians 4:6-7 (Be careful for nothing.)

• What difference does it make to know that God is with us in our difficulties?

• What steps can we take to seek "the peace of God" (Philippians. 4:7)?

• How can we keep our faith alive when our prayers are not answered as quickly as we would like, or in the way we had hoped?

B. God Will Provide

Philippians 4:19 (God shall supply all your need.)

Mosiah 2:20-21 (God is preserving you from day to day.)

D&C 104:14-18 (It is my purpose to provide for my saints.)

• How can trust in God's care keep us from despairing?

• What resources are available to help us through this time of difficulty?

• Why does the Lord speak so sharply of the need to help others (see D&C 104:18)?

C. My Heart Is Overwhelmed

Psalms 61:1-4 (Lead me to the rock that is higher than I.)

Alma 37:36-37 (Cry unto God for all thy support.)

D&C 24:8 (Be patient in afflictions, for I am with thee.)

• How have our difficulties caused family members to feel overwhelmed?

• What steps can we take to seek strength from God?

• How can we help each other be patient while we work things through?

D. One Day at a Time

Psalms 37:23-24 (Your steps are ordered by the Lord.)

Matthew 6:26-34 or *3 Nephi 13:26-34* (Take no thought for the morrow.)

D&C 58:3 (Ye cannot behold for now the design of your God.)

• What does it mean to take things one day at a time?

• How can we keep from worrying unduly about the future?

• What difference does it make to know that God is ordering our steps, even if we cannot see it now?

E. An Optimistic Outlook

Proverbs 12:25 (Heaviness in the heart maketh it stoop.)

Alma 33:23 (May your burdens be light through the joy of God's Son.)

D&C 68:6 (Be of good cheer, for I will stand by you.)

• Why is it important to retain an optimistic outlook?

• What "good words" can we offer each other during this difficult time (see Proverbs 12:25)?

• How can our relationship with the Savior lend hope and support?

F. In Every Thing Give Thanks

1 Thessalonians 5:18 (In every thing give thanks.)

Alma 7:23 (Return thanks for whatsoever ye receive.)

D&C 98:1-3 (Your afflictions shall work together for your good.)
• Despite our difficulties, what does our family still have to be thankful for?
• How can remembering our blessings help us confront our difficulties?
• How can we keep alive our faith that things will work out?

G. Remember Your Worth

Psalms 139:14 (I will praise thee, for I am wonderfully made.)
Philippians 4:13 (I can do all things through Christ.)
D&C 18:10 (The worth of souls is great in God's sight.)
• How can financial difficulties cause people to question their self-worth?
• How does knowing our value in God's eyes help us confront our difficulties?
• What talents, capabilities, and strengths do we have which will help us cope?

H. Support One Another

Galatians 6:2 (Bear ye one another's burdens.)
Moroni 7:45-47 (Cleave unto charity.)
D&C 108:7 (Strengthen your brethren.)
• How can family members share the new burdens occasioned by our difficulties?
• Why is it important to have charity for each other during this stressful time?
• What can we do to strengthen one another?

I. A Simpler Life

Proverbs 30:8 (Give me neither poverty nor riches.)
1 Timothy 6:6-8 (Having food and raiment let us be content.)
Alma 1:27 (The Lord's people lived simply and shared with others.)
• What steps can we take to simplify our lives and economize?
• Why is it a good idea to live simply all the time, not only during times of financial strain?
• How does living simply make it possible for us to do more to help others?

Discussions and Activities

A. Read or retell 2 Kings 4:1-7. Point out how the family in this story took steps to seek the Lord's help in overcoming financial difficulty. Discuss the questions: What steps can our family take to overcome our financial difficulty? How can we seek the Lord's assistance?

B. Read Proverbs 15:22 and 19:20. Discuss the questions: How might financial counseling or other financial assistance services be helpful to us? How can we seek the Spirit's guidance in deciding what action to take or whose help to seek?

C. Financial difficulties were a recurring problem for the early Saints. Consequently, several passages in Doctrine and Covenants contain advice and promises from the Lord regarding financial difficulties, especially debt:

• D&C 19:35 (Pay the debt; release thyself from bondage.)
• D&C 72:9-14 (Members can seek financial help from the bishop.)
• D&C 104:78-79 (The Lord promises to help the Saints pay their debts.)
• D&C 111:5 (I will give you power to pay your debts.)
• D&C 136:25 (If thou canst not pay, go straightway and tell thy neighbor.)

Discuss the questions: What difference does it make to know that our spiritual forebears also experienced financial difficulties? How might our family apply the principles in these passages to our own situation?

D. As part of the lesson, "A Simpler Life," read Exodus 20:17 (Mosiah 13:24). Discuss the question: In what ways does our society actually encourage its members to covet? How does coveting cause many people to get into financial troubles?

E. As a family, develop a plan for coping with your financial difficulties. Read and discuss Philippians 4:13. Lay your family's plan before the Lord, asking him for help, strength, and guidance.

F. Make a drawing of a tall rock surrounded by flood waters. Invite family members to label the flood waters with things that have caused them to feel overwhelmed during the family's financial difficulty: perhaps negative emotions, added stresses and worries, or new responsibilities they've had to take on. Then read Psalms 61:1-2. Draw your family members standing with the Savior on top of the rock, above the flood waters. (You could do a similar kind of activity with Matthew 8:23-26, depicting your family in a boat, with the Savior, in the middle of a storm-tossed sea.)

G. Read the counsel given to Emma Smith in D&C 25:5. Discuss the question: What can family members do to comfort one another during this difficult time?

H. In the case of a family who has lost their home, read Luke 9:57-58 and discuss the question: What difference does it make to realize that Jesus also knew what it was like to be without a home?

I. Family members who are having a difficult time coping may find it helpful to receive a priesthood blessing.

Spiritual Difficulties

Note: In the case of a family member who is breaking with the Church (see Lesson Idea E), it may be desirable to hold a family discussion on some of the topics below, rather than a family devotional.

Songs and Hymns
Press Forward, Saints (*Hymns* 81)
Lead, Kindly Light (*Hymns* 97)
Rock of Ages (*Hymns* 111)
Come unto Him (*Hymns* 114)
Come, Follow Me (*Hymns* 116)
Oh, May My Soul Commune with Thee (*Hymns* 123)
Where Can I Turn for Peace? (*Hymns* 129)
Be Still, My Soul (*Hymns* 124)
Love at Home (*Hymns* 294)
I Am a Child of God (*Hymns* 301, *Children's Songbook* 2)

Lesson Ideas
A. Doubts and Questions
Mark 9:23-24 (I believe; help thou mine unbelief.)
1 Nephi 10:17, 19 (They that diligently seek shall find.)
D&C 88:118 (Seek learning by study and also by faith.)
JS-H 1:8-13 (My mind was called up to serious reflection.)

• How is it possible for someone to believe and doubt at the same time (Mark 9:24)?

• In what way do our loved one's questions resemble those of Joseph Smith?

• How can we support our loved one in his/her search for answers?

B. Seeking Direction

Isaiah 42:16 (I will lead them in ways they have not known.)

Isaiah 48:17 or *1 Nephi 20:17* (God leadeth thee by the way thou shouldst go.)

D&C 78:17-18 (I will lead you along.)

• What unexpected—perhaps unwanted—turns has our loved one's life taken?

• How can we support our loved one in his/her search for new direction?

• What difference does it make to know that, whether or not we can see it, God is leading our loved one along?

C. Working through Repentance

Philippians 3:13-14 (Forgetting what is behind, I press toward the mark.)

Moroni 6:4-5 (That they might be remembered and nourished.)

D&C 133:16 (The Lord calleth all to repent.)

• What changes is our loved one working to make in his/her life?

• How can we support our loved one in making these changes?

• In what sense are we all undergoing a life-long repentance process?

D. Peace of Conscience

John 8:1-11 (Neither do I condemn thee.)

Enos 1:1-8 (My guilt was swept away.)

Mosiah 4:1-3 (They were filled with peace of conscience.)

D&C 24:2 (Thou art not excusable; nevertheless, go thy way.)

• What do these passages teach us about finding spiritual peace after transgression?

• When is guilt healthy, and when does it become counterproductive?

• How can we help our loved one move on with his/her life?

E. We Are Still Family

Jeremiah 31:3 (I have loved thee with an everlasting love.)
Moroni 7:45-48 (Pray for the pure love of Christ.)
D&C 38:27 (I say unto you, be one.)

• When a family member makes choices which other family members cannot accept, how can we preserve a sense of togetherness?

• What does it mean to love each other unconditionally?

• Why is unconditional love so difficult to practice?

Discussions and Activities

A. One natural reaction to a loved one's spiritual difficulties is fear—fear of the unfamiliar terrain into which the loved one may be heading, fear that the loved one will be lost, or fear that other family members may be led astray. Read 1 John 4:18 and D&C 50:41-42. Then reflect on the following questions:

• Why does John say, "He that feareth is not made perfect in love"?

• How can fear keep me from reacting constructively to my loved one's difficulties?

• How can my faith in the atonement—including the sealing power—help dispel fear that my loved one will be irretrievably lost?

B. As part of the lessons, "Doubts and Questions" or "Seeking Directions," ask each family member to come to the devotional with a scripture or a statement by a General Authority which addresses the question: How can we recognize the guidance of the Spirit?

C. Someone who is going through a period of doubt or questioning may find it helpful to study Alma 32:26-43. Reflect on the following questions in your journal:

Verses 26-28

• If faith is not to have a perfect knowledge, is it realistic to expect to find answers to all my questions?

• If I cannot find answers to all my questions, how can I decide what to believe?

• What do I desire to believe? Why do I desire to believe these things?

• When have I felt that something had "enlarg[ed] my soul" or "enlighten[ed] my understanding? What ideas, insights, or experiences have been "delicious" to me?

Verses 29-33

• The feelings Alma describes in v. 28 are what we usually call a testimony. Why does Alma say that a witness of this kind is not a perfect knowledge?

• According to Alma, what does a testimony make me sure of?

Verses 34-36

• According to these verses, in what sense is it accurate to say "I know" when I bear my testimony?

• In what sense is it not accurate?

Verses 37-43

• What does it mean to nourish the word?

• What does it mean for faith to bear fruit?

• Why does the search for knowledge require faith, diligence, patience, and long-suffering?

• According to Alma, when will I finally obtain perfect knowledge?

D. As part of the lessons, "Working through Repentance" or "Peace of Conscience," read 1 John 3:20. Discuss the questions: Why is it important not to get bogged down in self-recrimination? What is the most constructive approach to take when we know we have done something wrong?

E. Someone who is undergoing church discipline may find it helpful to reflect on the following passages of scripture: Psalms 145:8-9, 18; Romans 8:38-39; James 1:5; 3 Nephi 14:7-11; D&C 19:38-39. Why is it especially important that a person who has been separated from certain privileges of church membership continue to cultivate a strong personal relationship with God? What ways of approaching God are available to all people, regardless of their membership status?

F. As part of the lesson "Peace of Conscience," read Alma 42:29-31. Discuss the following questions:

• What does Alma mean when he tells Corianton to "let these things trouble you no more"?

• What might keep someone from letting God's justice have full sway in his/her heart?

• What might keep someone from letting God's mercy and long-suffering have full sway in his/her heart?

• Having just called Corianton to repent of a serious transgression, why would Alma then send him "to preach the word of God unto this people"?

G. As part of the lesson, "We Are Still Family," read D&C 130:2. Discuss the question: Notwithstanding our differences or disagreements, what kind of "sociality" do we want to prevail among family members?

H. Family members may worry about how to accept a loved one who has made choices they cannot accept. The following passages of scripture may be useful for reflection:

• Proverbs 17:17 (A brother is born for adversity, loveth at all times.)

• John 17:20-23 (That they may be made perfect in one.)

• Romans 12:10 (Be kindly affectioned one to another.)

• Romans 13:8 (He that loveth another hath fulfilled the law.)

• Galatians 5:14-15 (Take heed that ye be not consumed one of another.)

• 1 Thessalonians 3:12 (The Lord make you to abound in love.)

• 1 John 2:9-10 (He that loveth his brother abideth in the light.)

• 1 John 3:18-19 (Let us not love in word, but in deed.)

• 1 John 4:7-8 (Every one that loveth is born of God.)

• Alma 7:23-24 (Be gentle, full of patience and long-suffering.)

• 3 Nephi 11:29-30 (He that hath the spirit of contention is not of me.)

• 4 Nephi 1:15 (There was no contention because of the love of God.)

• D&C 112:11 (Be not partial towards thy brethren in love.)

• D&C 121:41-44 (By gentleness and by love unfeigned.)

I. When a loved one leaves the Church, it is natural for family members to experience grief—grief for the loss of a bond between themselves and their loved one, or grief for their shattered expectations of their loved one. Some of the devotional ideas in the section of this book titled "Loss of a Dream," may be applicable.

J. Depending on the circumstances, consider closing the devotional with a priesthood blessing for the one experiencing spiritual difficulties.

Marital Difficulties or Behavior Problems

Songs and Hymns

Father Up Above (*Children's Songbook* 23)
Where Love Is (*Children's Songbook* 138)
I Need Thee Every Hour (*Hymns* 98)
Be Still, My Soul (*Hymns* 124)
I Know That My Redeemer Lives (*Hymns* 136)
Let Us Oft Speak Kind Words (*Hymns* 232)
Love at Home (*Hymns* 294)
Home Can Be a Heaven on Earth (*Hymns* 298)
Love One Another (*Hymns* 308, *Children's Songbook* 136)

Lesson Ideas

A. Seeking Help and Guidance

Exodus 18:18 (This thing is too heavy for thee alone.)
Proverbs 15:22 (Without counsel purposes are disappointed.)
Alma 37:37 (Counsel with the Lord; he will direct thee.)

• How can outside help be useful in coping with family problems?

• Why do we need to use discernment in seeking outside help?

• How can we seek the Lord's guidance in deciding where to turn?

B. God Will Support Us

Psalms 46:1 (A very present help in trouble.)
Hebrews 4:15-16 (Come boldly to the throne of grace.)
Alma 36:3 (God will support us in all our troubles.)

• Why might having family problems cause people to feel ashamed or unworthy?

• What comfort do these passages offer people who feel this way?

• What steps can we take to seek God's help in resolving our family problems?

C. Learning to Change

Philippians 4:13-14 (Forgetting what is behind, reaching for what is before.)

3 Nephi 12:47 (Old things are done away, all have become new.)

D&C 50:40 (Ye are little children; ye must grow in grace.)

• Why does the fact that we are all growing make it unrealistic to hope that things can go back to the way they were "before"?

• What changes do we want to accomplish in our family life?

• How can we seek God's grace to help us make those changes?

D. Learning to Love

Titus 2:4 (Love within families is learned.)

Mosiah 4:15 (Teach them to love one another.)

D&C 121:41-44 (No influence but by love unfeigned.)

• We typically think of love as something we feel. What difference does it make to think of love as something we learn to do?

• How can we learn to be more effective spouses or parents?

• How can we apply the principles laid out in D&C 121 to our current difficulties?

E. Learning to Forgive

Ephesians 4:31-32 (Let all bitterness be put away from you.)

Moroni 7:47-48 (Pray that ye may be filled with charity.)

D&C 64:8-9 (Ye ought to forgive one another.)

• As we work to resolve our family problems, why is it important that we forgive?

• How might family members "seek occasion against one another" (D&C 64:8)?

• How can we overcome negative feelings towards one another?

F. Overcoming Contention

Proverbs 15:18 (One who is slow to anger appeaseth strife.)

Matthew 4:9 or *3 Nephi 12:9* (Blessed are the peacemakers.)

4 Nephi 1:15 (There was no contention; God's love dwelt in their hearts.)

• How is contention a sign that we need to learn new skills for relating to each other?
 • Would outside help be useful for making peace in our family?
 • How can we invite God's reconciling influence more fully into our home?

G. Pressing Forward

Isaiah 40:31 or *D&C 89:18-20* (Run and not be weary.)
Matthew 11:28 (Come unto me, all ye that labour.)
2 Nephi 31:19-20 (Press forward with steadfastness.)
 • What would it mean, in our circumstances, to rely wholly on Christ?
 • What would it mean to maintain a perfect brightness of hope?
 • How can we seek strength and comfort from the Savior when we feel worn out?

Discussions and Activities

A. Read 1 Nephi 17:48 and D&C 24:16. Reflect on the questions: What do these passages of scripture suggest about the importance of not "putting up" with violence or abuse? If there is violence in my home, how can I move to put an end to it? Where can I seek help?

B. There are multiple approaches to dealing with marital difficulties or behavior problems, and various resources available to help. Discuss the question: How can we seek the Spirit's guidance in deciding where to turn for help?

C. Read D&C 93:43. Discuss the questions: How is the whole family affected by the marital difficulties or behavior problems of one or some of its members? To what degree does resolving the problem require changes on the part of all family members?

D. Once you have decided what measures to take in working to resolve your family problem (self-help, counseling, and so on), read 2 Nephi 25:23. Discuss the question: How can we seek the Savior's grace in addition to these others measures?

E. If you are experiencing marital difficulties, read D&C 132:13-14. Reflect on the question: How can we tap more fully into the power of the restored gospel to make our marriage an enduring one?

If you are the parent of a child with behavior problems, read Malachi 4:5-6 (3 Nephi 25:5-6). Reflect on the question: How can we tap more fully into the power of the restored gospel to repair strained or broken bonds between parents and children?

F. Read 2 Nephi 2:26. Reflect on the following questions, perhaps in your journal: How should I respond when a loved one behaves in ways I cannot accept? How can I respect my loved one's agency while at the same time preserving my own well-being (and, if applicable, fulfilling my responsibilities as a parent)?

G. Read Matthew 7:3-5 (3 Nephi 14:3-5) and discuss the questions: Why is casting blame unhelpful in dealing with family problems? What is a more constructive way to approach our problem?

H. Read Luke 12:1-3 and D&C 50:7. Reflect on the questions: Why do people who are experiencing family problems often feel a need to create a facade of normalcy? Is this really helpful? What is the difference between preserving the family's privacy and creating an unhealthy atmosphere of secrecy?

I. Read Job 32:17-20. Reflect on the questions: Why is it important that family members deal with problems openly, rather than "bottling up" their feelings, frustrations, and concerns? What does it take to create a home environment where that kind of open communication can occur effectively and constructively?

J. Read D&C 31:2. Then reflect on the following questions in your journal: What blessings does my family enjoy in addition to our difficulties? How can remembering those blessings help me keep the difficulties in perspective? How do the blessings serve as a reminder that God is with us and supporting us?

K. Read Jeremiah 31:1. Discuss the question: What difference does it make to know that despite our difficulties, God is still our family's God?

L. Read D&C 130:2. Discuss the question: Why does it take work to create the kind of "sociality" or family relationships we want? In what sense is overcoming family problems a life-long task?

M. Read 1 Nephi 18:17-19. Reflect on the questions: How can family problems negatively affect the mental and physical health of family members? What steps can I take to preserve my health during this time?

N. In the spirit of 3 Nephi 18:21, consider praying, not that family members will change, but simply that they will be blessed. Reflect on the question: How can praying this way help me develop a more

Christlike love for my family members? How can it help me place my trust in God's will, rather than in my own?

O. After family members have discussed the process by which they are going to work to overcome their marital difficulties or behavior problems, read Psalms 127:1. In prayer, ask the Lord to assist you in the process of strengthening your family.

Divorce

Note: While it would be ideal to have both spouses present during the devotionals described below, that may not be possible or desirable, depending on the circumstances of the divorce.

Songs and Hymns

A Child's Prayer (*Children's Songbook* 12)
Heavenly Father, Now I Pray (*Children's Songbook* 19)
How Firm a Foundation (*Hymns* 85)
I Need Thee Every Hour (*Hymns* 98)
Cast Thy Burden upon the Lord (*Hymns* 110)
Come, Ye Disconsolate (*Hymns* 115)
Be Still, My Soul (*Hymns* 124)
Where Can I Turn for Peace? (*Hymns* 129)
I Am a Child of God (*Hymns* 301, *Children's Songbook* 2)

Lesson Ideas

A. God Will Heal Us

Psalms 147:3 (He healeth the broken in heart.)
Malachi 4:2 or *3 Nephi 25:2* (The Son shall arise with healing in his wings.)
Alma 7:11-12 (He will take upon him our pains.)
• How have family members been wounded by the divorce?
• What difference does it make to know that Christ shares our pains?
• How can we draw on the Savior's healing power as we press forward with our lives?

B. God Will Comfort Us

Matthew 11:28 (Come unto me, all ye that labor.)

John 14:18 (I will not leave you comfortless.)
D&C 61:36 (I have not forsaken you.)
- In what sense is the end of a marriage like a death?
- How has the divorce caused family members to feel abandoned, betrayed, or overwhelmed?
- What steps can we take to seek the Savior's comfort?

C. God Will Lead Us Along
Isaiah 42:16 (I will lead them in paths they have not known.)
Revelation 7:17 (The Lamb shall lead them and wipe away all tears.)
2 Nephi 4:20-21 (My God hath led me through mine afflictions.)
- What decisions need to be made as a result of the divorce?
- How can we open ourselves to the Spirit's guidance as we make these decisions?
- What difference does it make to know that, however uncertain the future, God is leading us along?

D. God Will Be Our Support
Isaiah 40:28-29 (He giveth power to the faint.)
Alma 37:36-37 (Cry unto God for all thy support.)
D&C 24:8 (Be patient in afflictions, for I am with thee.)
- What new burdens have been placed on family members as a result of the divorce?
- How can we find spiritual strength to cope with these burdens?
- Why is it important to be patient as we struggle to adapt?

E. God Will Help Us Forgive
Ephesians 4:31-32 (Let all bitterness be put away from you.)
3 Nephi 11:29-30 (Contentions should be done away.)
Moroni 7:47-48 (Pray that ye may be filled with charity.)
- How has the divorce been an occasion of bitterness and contention?
- Why is it so important—and so difficult—to let go of these negative feelings?
- How can God help us learn to forgive?

F. We Have God's Promises

Psalms 119:49-50 (Thou hast caused me to hope; this is my comfort.)

2 Peter 1:2-4 (We have been given exceeding great promises.)

D&C 78:17-18 (Be of good cheer; the riches of eternity are yours.)

• What hopes had our family placed in this marriage?

• What promises does God extend regardless of marital or family status?

• How do those promises provide hope and comfort in the aftermath of the divorce?

G. Parents and Children

1 Thessalonians 3:12 (The Lord make you to abound in love.)

Mosiah 4:13-15 (Parents should teach and provide for their children.)

D&C 83:4 (All children have claim upon their parents.)

• How will family members' involvement in one another's lives change as a result of the divorce?

• How does the divorce affect the love between parents and children?

• In what sense will both parents continue to work together to raise their children?

Discussions and Activities

A. Discuss the practical changes that will come to your family's life as a result of the divorce. D&C 88:119 ("Organize yourselves; prepare every needful thing") could serve as a basis for this discussion. Pay special attention to assuring children that they are not the cause of the divorce, that they are still loved by both parents, and that they need not feel guilty for continuing to feel loyal to both parents.

B. Invite family members to reflect on their fears or anxieties about the divorce, either silently or out loud. Read Isaiah 41:10. Discuss the question: How does a close relationship with God help us find the strength and confidence to face our fears?

C. Invite each family member to create a drawing or collage depicting his/her feelings about the divorce. After the drawings are complete, read and discuss Psalms 25:16-17. Title each drawing, "Turn thee unto me, for I am desolate." Have family members hang their drawings near their beds, where they will see them during personal prayers.

D. Make a drawing of a tall rock surrounded by flood waters. Invite family members to label the flood waters with things that have made them feel anxious or overwhelmed in the aftermath of the divorce. Then read Psalms 61:1-2. Draw your family members standing with the Savior on top of the rock, above the flood waters.

E. Read Jeremiah 31:1 and discuss the following questions: In what sense are we still a family, albeit of a different kind? What difference does it make to know that despite changes in our family's structure, God is still our family's God?

F. Read Galatians 3:26. Discuss the question: With our family life as we knew it coming to an end, what difference does it make to know that, whatever else happens, we will always belong to God's family?

G. Read D&C 89:18-20. Explain how important it is that family members take good care of themselves physically, as well as spiritually, while they cope with the divorce.

H. Explain that family members may feel a need for outside support as they cope with the divorce. Discuss where family members might turn for support, or a listening ear, outside the family itself.

I. Explain that divorce involves a grieving process, as family members mourn the loss of their hopes and expectations for family life. See the section of this book titled "Loss of a Dream."

J. Depending on the circumstances, the divorcing couple may find it helpful to formally mark the end of their relationship by meeting to bid each other best wishes in their future lives.

K. In the spirit of 3 Nephi 18:21, resolve to keep mentioning all family members in your prayers.

Bibliography

Ludlow, Daniel H., ed. *Encyclopedia of Mormonism.* 4 vols. New York: Macmillan, 1992.

Melchizedek Priesthood Personal Study Guide. Salt Lake City: The Church of Jesus Christ of Latter-day Saints, 1994.

Sill, Sterling W. *The Glory of the Sun.* Salt Lake City, Bookcraft, 1961.

Smith, Joseph Fielding. *Doctrines of Salvation.* 3 vols. Salt Lake City: Bookcraft, 1955.

Widtsoe, John A., comp. *Discourses of Brigham Young.* Salt Lake City: Deseret Book, 1941.

Index

About the Author

The son of convert parents, John Charles Duffy is the first member of his family born into The Church of Jesus Christ of Latter-day Saints. He served a mission in the Dominican Republic from 1991-1993; he returned to that country in 1997 as an education volunteer in a program serving a cluster of isolated villages.

He holds a Bachelor of Arts in English from Brigham Young University, and a Master of Arts in English from the University of Utah, where he has been an associate instructor since 1998.

John currently serves as an officer in the Association for Mormon Letters. His work has appeared in literary journals, as well as in BYU's *The Restored Gospel* and *Applied Christianity*. In addition, he is the author of *My Heart Cries Out to Thee*, a book of inspirational devotions published by Horizon Publishers.